My Hidden Family

Judith M. Glover.

My Hidden Family

My Journey of Discovery, Decision and Deceit

JUDITH M. GLOVER

THE CHOIR PRESS

First published in the United Kingdom in 2020 by
The Choir Press

ISBN 978-1-78963-127-2

Cover designed by Margaret Southgate

Contents

———

Foreword

———

It is strange how absurd objects suddenly affect you – I stopped washing the breakfast pots and as I held up my old wooden spoon I suddenly remembered with what immense pride I had bought this inanimate object years ago whilst adding to my 'bottom drawer'. This is an old adage hardly applicable in modern days, but to me in the late 1960s, with little money available, every item added to my collection then was enjoyed with such pride. In post-war Britain it was not the 'throwaway' era of today. It was part of the key which would open my world to a new life. I held a spoon partly worn away, which had lost its colour, done plenty of hard work but was still hanging in there and being useful now and then. A bit like me, really!

Once we start reminiscing it can be dangerous, for then the mind takes over. A new laptop arrives with all sorts of information already stored in its memory – do we as newborn babies arrive with the same sort of built-in paraphernalia? Certainly new infants have the blueprint for their future development regarding their appearance, capabilities, intelligence and adult height, etc., but even that preparation will be influenced by the environment they will grow up in and people surrounding them. Genealogy is fascinating, and to scan someone's personal mind computer is equally interesting, as it encompasses its owner's thought processes and personality in its handling, content and the way that information is stored from a lifetime of experiences.

Computers do not stay with a human being an entire lifetime, so why has that simile presented itself to me? Untrue things told and believed during childhood, miscellaneous items which are rubbish at the bottom of a drawer kept for their sentimental value and useless accumulated treasures travel alongside us through many years. It is not possible, though, for human beings to throw away deep-set mental images in the memory bank, and whether pleasant or unpleasant they walk alongside us like a shadow all through our lives.

Once more it is much the same with the people around us from childhood or adulthood, for however brief the meeting or when it happened, a tiny bit of that person always remains with us. Any minute conversation leaves its imprint in the same way childish thoughts, questions or superstitions take their tiny bit of brain space to remain in a brain computer file, ready to emerge when least expected or to bring déjà vu experiences in the adult mind.

So why, as the years bring fulfilment of maturity (which in some cases does not occur until the late fifties), do all these little shreds of minutiae suddenly become important and part of the bigger picture? Surely a lot of this rubbish should have been offloaded into a recycle bin years ago, but no – still it is there to haunt, bring back every last vestige of every experience in a life, and with age reaches out to grab and wrest the very heart and soul of the bodily occupant, only taking something as ridiculous and insignificant as an old wooden spoon to become the key to that inward spiral of thought that stirs memories to the surface.

We believe our minds are selective and that we control them, but every so often they pop a tiny bit of memory out in the strangest circumstances in life's journey. Whether we think a person has influenced us or not, given time spent with an individual we begin to mimic words, accents, little gestures or expressions and frequently retain the ones we particularly like so that they then become part of ourselves. A stirring-in of additives?

Our mind triggers shockwaves, which make ever-expanding circles like a pebble thrown into a pond, and we write memorabilia on our brain computer just as if someone had inserted it via a USB port. However, unlike a memory stick we cannot remove that data completely from our memory.

I make no apology for adding another bone-shaking biographical story to the millions already in circulation, gathering dust no doubt. If it gives grandchildren an insight as to how someone's life was, stirs memories or brings a smile to one person's face, it has done its job. If it is thrown away or gathers dust so be it – to the writer it will have been therapeutic!

Wooden spoons are stirrers. Is there some sort of trigger in humans which does the same job to rouse the mind – a sort of brain shaker? Good and bad, hurtful and constructive, silly or sensible. In the human computer there are files stacked with dormant information containing chapter upon chapter of illogical, happy, tragic, memorable and changing software. Billions have taken such rich memories, knowledge and information with them at the end of their lives, and how tragic they did not leave more of these things behind for us to learn. Every particle of self as a human being, built over years of experience and life. So, let those most interesting and sometimes quite bizarre chapters of mine be opened and stirred with the poor old wooden spoon for posterity to be copied and pasted into the mind computers of descendants who, hopefully, will be interested in their ancestor's personal 'Once Upon a Time'.

My own story began with nothing – no knowledge even of who I 'really' was. My mixing bowl is filled with such improbable content and unexpected results I will never really know how it all turned out, as it included so many ingredients. What did turn out was unbelievable ...

For my wonderful families – ALL of them,
for without them I would not be
who I am today.

CHAPTER 1

Childhood

———

'How do you come to terms with what you have discovered?' This is a question I have been asked many times over the past few years, and there is no clear answer. I could reply that it has been like a roller-coaster, daunting, unexpected, mind-blowing or simply incredible! All those things. I guess the best explanation is to say that it almost feels as I am in some sort of time-warp and that it is all happening to someone else where I am simply the onlooker.

The discoveries I have made definitely relate to me, but who am I? Well, that is the question, or rather the question which has haunted me for the biggest part of my life. It is almost as if I am looking into some sort of window, or into a television set where the participants have been put into a soap opera, where the weaving in and out, the ups and downs, have happened to one of the characters in the soap – but without foul language or physical violence! But – no. It is me to whom this has all happened, and which has turned into an intriguing and completely unforeseen life story. It is an enormous jigsaw puzzle, some pieces of which can never be found or put together, for it is too late.

The old axiom 'Truth is stranger than fiction' cannot be denied, particularly with my story – the majority of which took over sixty-eight years to discover as, theoretically, until actual records of me were discovered I could have gone anywhere I wished and started a new life altogether.

A new life is a blank page to be written on, and normally

Possibly the first photograph at about 20 months old.

begins with tenderness, pride and nurture, but as we see from modern television series such as *Long Lost Family*, and *Who Do You Think You Are*, it has become apparent to millions of people all over the world that a lot of people never *really* discover their true heritage. Sometimes an individual's first 'page' begins a little later than the rest of their contemporaries. It is easy to track down information in our computers, but not our brains. No one has yet been able to remember their own birth or the first few years of their lives apart from what input is given by relatives, and those memories we 'think' we remember.

Everyone remembers bits and pieces from our earliest lives; perhaps from the ages of two or three, which are snatches of tiny unrelated incidents which our mind has photographed into our life story. However, there will always be one more definite memory which we remember from around the ages of four or five, and that is where my earliest positive situation is retrieved from.

*

'Today we have a new little girl amongst us,' Miss French announced animatedly, and I, along with the thirty-odd other five-year-olds lined up in the ancient school cloakroom looked around with interest to see who the latest victim was. A murmur went around, as no new faces could be seen, and then suddenly all eyes were on me, squirming on one leg near the ancient stone sinks in the school cloakroom. Why was she looking at me – I wasn't a new pupil?

Being of a very timid nature even then, my young brain shrank from being the centre of attention, and then enlightenment dawned as Miss French pointed out to everyone that I was wearing my new National Health glasses with white frames, the wire of which wrapped right round the back of my ears and – over the years as my bones grew – caused deep trenches at the back of my skull!

For the first time in my very sheltered life, the misgivings of being in the spotlight swept through me, and of course it was not long before the usual nicknames of 'Specky Four Eyes', 'Olive Oil' and various rhymes about 'Girls who wear glasses' etc. were being chanted – even in 1953 young kids could be callous! Bearing in mind it had only been a short time since Miss French had picked up that I was copying gobbledegook from the little boy sitting next to me in class, and had therefore placed me on the front row of shame for 'copying', it soon became apparent that the rubbish I was now attempting to copy meant that I could not see the blackboard.

This of course was soon revealed to my mother, and resulted in her dragging me, loudly crying, into the Big Unknown – i.e. the optician's shop – where without let, hindrance or explanation of what was about to happen I was bribed with a sweet to go in and sit down. It never seemed to occur to my mum or gran that an explanation of what was going to happen to me would help!

Following the trauma of a first eye-test I remember thinking at the time I had got off pretty lightly, particularly as

3

Photo by Dad shortly after being taken from Kilrie Children's Home.

great wonders of the world were being revealed in pure clarity rather than the familiar blurred surroundings. I had recently been taken with the rest of the infant school to the local Ritz Cinema to see the Queen's coronation, and hadn't had a clue about what was on the big screen as it was all a blur, but of course was too young to explain this to anyone at that time. I well remember being terrified of Miss French (and, incidentally, everyone else who was outside my little personal home cocoon), but in later years I came to think of her as a benefactress, being the person who opened the world to me in more ways than one!

This entire experience, trivial as it might seem to modern-day children, had pointed me out as being 'different' from other children, as no one else in my class wore spectacles, and that is why such a memory still exists now decades later, because knowing I was somehow dissimilar to other children of my group was only the beginning of that realisation. This was not in any physical way, but as the years progressed my upbringing was so claustrophobic and unusual I retreated into myself and a fantasy world, where my dolls, teddies and playthings became more real to me than anything in the 'outside' world.

My dad was wonderful. He had taught me to read long before I started school, as after he had returned home from work and eaten his evening meal he would sit me on his knee and help me to build and spell out lovely long words from his evening newspaper. A man of great patience, I followed him around like a little shadow, and in later years when I asked him how he had managed to cope with my persistent questions and adoration, his reply was that if he had been bad-tempered with me, then I would have grown up to be bad-tempered, too. He and I had a lovely bond all through my childhood, as we two were definitely on the 'outside' of our minimalistic family, which consisted simply of myself, Dad, Mum and Gran.

Gran was my mother's mother, and had lived with my parents ever since she lost her husband just prior to the outbreak of the Second World War. This was the total extent of our 'family' as I knew it then. Just the four of us.

Of course, my dad served in the army and was present at the D-Day landings, but when he returned home in 1945 Gran had been living with Mum throughout the war years and she remained in the matrimonial home even after his return. This resulted in the situation that Mum and Gran were 'joined at the hip', and Dad was the rank outsider – later on to be joined by me. Never once did I hear him complain, but his life thereafter was at the behest of two very Victorian, self-righteous and opinionated ladies. I do not mean this in a cruel or disrespectful way, for I had a good mother and grandmother, but Gran definitely ruled the roost and this explains a lot of why my childhood progressed in the way it did.

Both ladies had served with the Red Cross during the war years, and therefore considered they knew 'everything' there was to be known about illnesses. Doctors were *never* consulted unless it was absolutely essential, and home remedies were the order of the day. (The reason for my white-coat syndrome?) It is very difficult to disagree with people who 'know everything', which Dad and I both grew to accept as they were one hundred percent rigid in their opinions. They were never wrong and were definitely never keen on the 'male sex'!

I never knew what was said or what went on behind the scenes. Being a child, I was to be seen and not heard right up to the age of twenty-two when I married, but I would imagine Dad gave up somewhere along the way of trying to win Mum to himself. It never happened. Even when I was married and had left home the regime of authoritarian bossing and interfering never ceased, and I never had the ability to go against their wishes – for fear of what? I cannot even answer that, but it was completely instilled in me. Had my husband and my in-laws not been the gentle, lovely, tolerant and understanding people they were, several World Wars would have broken out over the years to come!

This duo of Mum and Gran was very secretive. It was a situation whereby any tiny incident in a morning before I left for school would have blown up out of all proportion by the time I returned home, as it had been mulled over and talked about throughout the day. Neither of them ever went out to work – they didn't like to socialise. Likewise, Dad gave up his gardening and photographic clubs at work as he was continuously nagged about not coming straight home for his meal, and his local Saturday football team lost his patronage when I was around seven years old as, upon his returning home when the weather was inclement, he would face a barrage of how if he caught pneumonia by standing out in the freezing cold they were *not* going to nurse him. Eventually, as he said, it was like Chinese water torture, and therefore easier to stop going all together.

I record these events not through malice, for it was what it was, but simply as an explanation of how things were at home

With Dad at Charlesworth, aged around 2½.

all the way through my childhood. It would be difficult for many people from a more (shall I say?) 'normal' home life to understand the rules and regulations of my formative years and the restrictive and absolutely overpowering control of my life history. Mum and Gran's 'secret society' relationship meant many topics were taboo, and most certainly things were never explained to me. I was to be 'seen but not heard'. My mind and thoughts were totally theirs in the early days. In the house where I spent my childhood there were two downstairs rooms known as the 'back room' and the 'front room', the latter of which was the best room where the adults would rest in an evening, and I would play in the former room on my own – quietly. If I made a whimper or a murmur I would be told that 'If your dad was ill upstairs you would have to be quiet!' And so I never learnt to shout or scream like many of the other children at school. My surroundings were quiet and ladylike. Especially 'ladylike'. Protocol and demeanour were tantamount.

Bodies. Ah yes – anything physical. One hundred percent taboo. When we first moved to my childhood home in Hyde when I was almost five years old, there were two bedrooms upstairs, and no indoor bathroom. The toilet was in a little shed across the back yard. I therefore shared one of the bedrooms with my gran at first, which I well remember, and learnt from her early on the trick of getting undressed under my nightie. NO flesh on view whatsoever. I grew up terribly ashamed of my own body, as I was taught it was not a nice thing at all even to think about. At around the age of eight my dad split the larger front bedroom into two with a little passage at the side leading to my little 'room', and in which there was a lidded bath. I think Dad was the only person who ever used that bath, as the regime in our household was to have a 'wash down'. Much more acceptable!

Gran had been a tailoress, and she made the most beautiful clothes – all my dresses, school uniforms and heavy winter coats were made by her, and she knitted jumpers for everyone. She was also an accomplished needlewoman and enjoyed embroidery and crochet, making the loveliest things. I was therefore never allowed to choose clothes for myself, and when at around the age of eleven I saw a pretty dress in a shop which I ventured to say I liked, Mum and Gran were most offended at my ingratitude.

From childhood I was taught all these crafts and I remember my grandmother being a good and patient teacher. I used to watch her making garments on her treadle sewing machine and, childlike, tried to copy her when my dad brought me home a miniature Singer sewing machine which sewed 'real' stitches. I can never remember Mum attempting to knit or sew. Throughout the next fifty or sixty years I came to realise what an insecure person she was; I suspect that my gran had very high expectations of her daughter and when Mum could not meet Gran's standards and was continually criticised she simply stopped trying. As obedience was my forté, I would not have even considered going against Gran's wishes or tutorage, but I loved learning all those things.

Certainly, Gran was the one who was always busy – cooking, writing to penfriends, sewing, knitting, making clothes for herself, Mum and I, putting scrapbooks together or reading her weekly magazines such as 'People's Friend', which I remember well. She was also the one who, every Sunday, insisted we take a 'Sunday walk' in the countryside or to a park.

These two ladies never made friends outside of the home. Whenever we moved house they would seem to be friendly with the new neighbours – for a very short time anyway. What happened then I do not know, but they did not wish anyone outside the home to intrude in any way or know any of their business. This was not unusual in the post-war years when people and their private lives were just that – private. Mum and Gran, however, took this to a completely different level!

It is really strange now, in current times, to realise how everything under the sun is discussed openly and above board. Young people now need to be 'streetwise' and aware of what is going on around them to keep them safe, but in my somewhat very restricted childhood it was deemed quite unnecessary to explain to or discuss anything at all with me. Hindsight has always been a wonderful thing, and it is a pity we who are older did not have this wonderful gift when we were young, but I definitely grew up aware of nothing but the closeted rooms of our home, the relative freedom of our reasonably large garden, the toys I shared my life with and the comings and goings to school where I grew unhappier as the years went by. It seemed as though I was in some sort of parallel existence to my schoolfriends, and the extent of my complete world was within my home.

Surprisingly, I certainly held my own at school and was always in the top groups, but that was not through trying or encouragement. I was blissfully unaware that one had to do their best at school – all I ever wanted was to go home back to

First visit to Father Christmas at Lewis's in Manchester, Aged 3.

my private and dreamlike existence to pursue my imaginative games, thoughts and stories. Needless to say that is probably why I have such a vivid imagination. Mum and Gran would not hesitate to keep me off school if they wished to – say – go to Manchester for the day, or if they wanted to go and visit someone who lived two bus rides away. They wouldn't have got away with it now, but in those days no one was going to tell them what they could and couldn't do!

Of course, I did have some special friends – two of them actually, who were deemed 'suitable' to come to tea a few times and to play with me in the garden where Dad had built a little summerhouse. This brought great fun and lazy summer afternoons playing 'house'. I was also given a birthday party each year, when around eight classmates would be asked to tea, which was overseen from start to finish by Mum and Gran, of course, to make sure no one acted inappropriately or in less than a ladylike manner. Gran would make me a lovely party dress and use rags to make ringlets in my hair, which was usually plaited to escape the horror of … don't mention it … nits! Had I ever come home with those little visitors all hell would have broken loose! Thankfully, and probably due to Gran's very tight plaiting, it never happened. I had to suffer those plaits from the age of five to fifteen as there was no way my hair could be loose apart from on rare party days.

At Christmas I always awoke to a pillowcase at the foot of my bed bulging with intriguing and exciting parcels. I always received a tin oven with miniature pans, a doll or teddy-bear (Gran made me two lovely teddy-bears out of old coats), a paintbox, a tin of sticky sweets and lots of other little items, and I was very lucky indeed. I was never allowed to decorate the Christmas tree – that was Gran's job – but I can remember helping her make silver 'bells' out of shiny bottle tops.

Going forward a very long time to when my mum and Gran died, I realised that in their long lives of eighty-two and eighty-six years respectively, I had never held an 'adult' conversation with either of them. They were inextricably bound together and always treated me in a way of telling me what I was to do – and not always how to do it. They seemed to take for granted that I knew about things (important or not) without any teaching, and questions from me were never answered without prevarication.

Obviously everything was discussed between them all day long, as they were closeted in the house together on their own, just venturing out to do necessary shopping, etc. Although I could talk to Dad about many subjects, I never asked any personal questions, as from all three the reply would only have been 'ask no questions and you'll be told no lies'. Dad, given the chance, would have been far more approachable as I grew older had it not been for the influence of his wife and mother-in-law, but that is how it was, and I had no inkling whatsoever of what was going to unfold in my life as the years rolled by!

CHAPTER 2

Not Understanding

The passing of years brings progress in many ways and that is how the world develops, of course. Post-war children, such as myself, grew up in a very different environment than the one we have now, and some things are for the better – but others are not. My generation learnt to respect their belongings, which were frequently in short supply, and even things like old nails, string, paper and suchlike had to be carefully 'recycled'. That word is used frequently now of course, but in a very different context to the current 'throw-way' regime.

From the ages of five to fourteen we lived in the same little house, which was quite a long time considering Mum and Gran's history in terms of moving around. I remember so much about it and the happy times I had there playing in the garden, the summerhouse, the little yard with a huge stone plinth (never knew what it was for), where I would put jars of bluebells after our Sunday walks. Obviously we had to stay in one place because of the infant and junior schools I attended, which were only a very short walk away down a narrow passageway entered from the back gate of our garden. There were no roads to cross, and it was very safe from that point of view. It was also where I learnt to roller-skate and play on my scooter alone for hours on end. Today it would be deemed extremely unsafe, garden walls or fences on one side and the brick walls of Hyde United Football Ground on the other. I was frequently 'checked out' by Mum and Gran, naturally to make sure I wasn't getting up to anything untoward.

At around the age of seven, Mum and Gran began to tell me something *very* special. They said I had been adopted as a baby, and that I had been especially chosen. At that age it went right over my head and meant nothing whatsoever. But yes – I had been especially chosen but was 'never to tell anyone, ever, about it'. So, at around eight or nine years of age I knew I was 'special', but was also to be ashamed of it.

The only recollections I have at around that time, apart from the school routine, which was growing more difficult for me each year, are that I was expected to go for a 'medical' examination at a school clinic once or twice a year, which Mum did *not* appreciate. How I hated it as, of course, it meant stripping down to my vest – in front of a stranger, too! Mum was bad enough, as she virtually averted her eyes.

On one occasion the name 'Judith Ashton' was shouted out, and my mother went quite mad – she marched up to the reception desk where heated words were exchanged. Of course, I did not realise it referred to me, as my name was 'Judith Boothman'. How I hated those appointments, and I never received any explanation as to why I had to go there in the first place. Mum did not tell me why she was so angry either, and the memory soon faded, only to return many years later when I was attempting to make sense of many things.

Another memory I have – which I can remember on two or three occasions, was when a little black Ford car would draw up at our front door. That was a very unusual occurrence in the 1950s, as although we lived on a main road there were not too many vehicles around, and certainly none came to our house. At these times, Mum and Gran would fly into a panic, whereupon I would be sent off to play either in the garden or the back room. They made it quite clear this was not a situation they were happy with, and as usual they told me nothing.

After a suitable interval of time when a very tall lady had been shown into the front room and the door closed, I could hear the murmur of them talking. Shortly afterwards, Mum would come for me and I was taken into the room to stand in front of this lady, who was called Miss Bissett-Smith. She had a lisp but was very well-spoken indeed. She kindly asked me how I was getting on at school, would tell me how tall I was growing, and on a couple of occasions she brought me a little gift. One of them was a weaving set and the other a dolly bobbin set (which I still have). After the lady had left, of course I asked Mum and Gran why she had brought me a present (it was not my birthday, Christmas or Easter!), and they just said it was courtesy. The front room was like the Holy of Holies, whereby nothing that was discussed in there was explained to me.

The first time I realised things were not quite the same at home for me as they were for other little girls, was at school when a classmate called Joyce was talking about being 'adopted'. Two other little girls chimed in with the same news so, of course (despite the dire warnings I had received), I told them I was also adopted. However, upon saying how much I hated those medicals they all looked at me strangely, as none of them had experienced such things. That seemed quite odd, but at such a tender age I did not think anything more about it.

And so the years rolled by, but nothing much changed within my 'perfect' little world. I continued to play on my own for the majority of the time, and when we acquired a Bush television set there were even more things to imagine and 'play out' in my little sanctuary.

My 'Nemesis' at this stage of my life was food. Or lack of it. Why, how or when this problem began I have no idea, but I know Mum and Gran had a real problem trying to get me to eat. My dad seemed to think that as a baby I had been given a drink of milk which was too hot and had burnt my mouth, but

At Southport Pier with Gran, aged five.

whether that was what instigated it I shall never know. I simply found food horrible, and can remember feeling physically sick when, say, a roast dinner meal was placed in front of me. Gran was a superb cook and from what I can remember she did the majority of the cooking, and as was the rule in those days the midday meal was the main meal of the day. I think my mum was really concerned. I tried school dinners, and they were even worse, so they were stopped as it was a waste of money.

It seems I grew up on the few things I *would* eat: jam butties, porridge and sweet stuff. Because of this – and it could have been me simply being difficult – Mum always gave me anything I *would* eat, regardless of whether or not it was nutritious. Obviously, Mum and Gran got very angry with me, but it made things worse as I genuinely did not feel able to swallow the (albeit delicious, I realise now) meals they cooked for themselves. Mum actually made 'sugar' butties for me in an attempt to get me to eat something.

I was not allowed to have school milk or orange juice, and there was quite a furore about this in the infant school, as I remember both Mum and Gran coming in with me and complaining that those items were 'bad' for me. Orange juice was too acidic, and milk was not acceptable either. I suspect they themselves could not digest these items. Goodness knows how I managed to grow into a reasonably healthy adult in the end, but certainly I did not have more than anyone else's fair share of colds, coughs or contagious children's illnesses. I suspect it was a daily dose of 'Virol', which supplied the vitamins I needed, and the spoonfuls of which I loved! Having both been nurses during the war, it surprises me even now to realise why the two ladies did not know more about a child's needs regarding food. But of course they knew everything, didn't they?

My two closest friends, Ann and Lynne, who were occasionally invited to tea at our house, invited me on a return visit to their homes at some point. I was only asked once though, as their mothers did not know what to do with me regarding a meal, and I was so shy and nervous they didn't know how to even talk to me. I simply was not used to visiting friends' houses, but it must have been embarrassing for them.

My schooldays were tempered with – in a way – 'Big Brother'. Everything I did and said was overseen by my two matriarchs. Whilst at junior school I was always warned I must wear my hat and coat at playtimes. This came to a head one very hot summer's day when the cloakroom was out of bounds, as it was not considered outside clothing was necessary. Unfortunately, it was one of the days when Mum and Gran had been shopping in town and hid themselves behind the school wall to ensure I was doing what I was told. (This event was a random and fairly regular occurrence).

When they saw me running around in my summer frock with no coat and hat they marched into the headmaster and – believe me – it was made certain by teachers after that to make sure I donned the correct outdoor wear!

Looking back at old photos, this situation reminds me of an old black and white picture taken when I was five years old at Southport. I am sitting on the front row watching a Punch and Judy Show (couldn't see it properly of course, pre-glasses!) and I am the only child in that photograph resplendent with hat, coat, white socks and sandals. All the other children – it obviously being a hot day – were in shorts or summer dresses and running around in bare feet. Mind you, Dad always wore a shirt, tie and jacket, even in a heatwave; being dressed 'correctly' was of tantamount importance.

Gran, Mum and Dad had a few 'close' friends – none of them relatives but whom I would call aunties and uncles. One couple had become friends through Dad where he worked, two couples were Mum's girlhood friends from school, and another couple had met Mum and Gran at whist drives held at the local church, when we lived in Charlesworth. (We lived there from my turning two until I was almost five). I really loved these aunties and uncles, but once again everything was very hush-hush when they visited us, or we them. They all lived on the Salford side of Manchester, and it was a two-bus ride in those days – firstly into Manchester and then out on another bus into Salford.

Auntie Marjorie and Uncle Tom lived in Pendlebury, and whenever we visited them we would be given a light sandwich refreshment, and then I was expected to go and wash up in the kitchen. Looking back I suspect this was their time to talk and for 'news' about me to be relayed. The same was true when we visited the other friends. They must all have known about my situation, but never a word was breathed or referred to.

Like all children, despite being told not to ask questions, of course I did. I can remember asking Mum and Gran on several occasions what being adopted meant, and they did explain that the lady who gave birth to me could not keep me. So far so good. However, upon trying to get more information when I was around eight or nine years old, I received so many different explanations I could never make any sense of it. Amongst other things I was told my birth mother had died, gone abroad, abandoned me, not wanted me, or any other concoction they could think of. Maybe they did not know. The same happened when I asked about my 'first' dad. He was either a doctor, had died, gone to live abroad, or been someone bad. It was a matter of 'take your pick', but it didn't matter to me for I had a good home, lots of lovely toys and a wonderful Dad.

Mum arranged for me to have piano lessons with a music teacher who lived across the road from us, and at the age of nine I attended for nine months. I have no idea why the lessons stopped, maybe I would not practice, or perhaps it was too expensive, but it was sufficient to enable me to read music and self-teach myself for the rest of my life. I am very grateful for that.

My childhood wasn't a 'Disney' sort of home, but on a similar level, as nothing 'bad' was ever talked about, the outside world was never discussed. I had no idea how other children lived or played with their brothers or sisters, or how their parents hugged or loved them. I knew nothing about the daily news, which was banned from me, and no idea of how the world functioned. Life was beautiful with no difficulties.

Mine wasn't a total 'arm's length' situation emotionally, but I do not remember being cuddled or cosseted in any way. I probably was as a baby, but it was the 'stiff upper lip' syndrome when something went wrong. You did not trouble anyone but simply got on with it and sorted it out yourself. The only person I felt really cared was my dad, but even he only expected a peck of a kiss on the forehead when I went up to bed in the years I was growing up. Even as an adult a quick duty peck on the cheek given to Mum and Gran was the norm. To be fair, that is the generation they came from, and is how it was for many people of my generation. They were not in any way tactile, emotions were not discussed, and nor were many other things which I should have been told about and educated in. Really I was dreadfully vulnerable and unwordly, but as a child I was very happy and felt quite secure, not realising life could be any different. If I *did* have any thoughts about a future, it was that it would always be just as it was then, without any changes.

Looking back I do not know, now, how I got through school. As the years rolled by it is obvious to me looking back

Aged 9 with Mum and Dad.

that not only was I bullied because of the way I looked from around eight or nine years old, but also because I was so isolated. My shoulder-length hair was pulled tightly back into plaits, my NHS round-rimmed spectacles were ugly and my second front teeth were very prominent – in fact I could never close my mouth properly. 'Olive Oil' was the best description of all, as I was also growing tall very fast and was extremely thin. I bore no resemblance whatsoever to my parents, and Mum and Gran seemed to be quite oblivious of how different things *could* have been.

Dental care was nil. Mum had suffered a 'bad experience' once having a tooth extracted, with the result that we never, ever, crossed the threshold of a dentist's surgery. Her teeth were always bad, and I don't think anyone knew about orthodontic treatment either. During these years I became even more withdrawn and scared of other children, and at the age of ten when I moved into the top class at junior school, and for the first time had a male teacher, life hit the bottom big time.

This teacher had been an ex-army sergeant, and his regime was one of fear. Every Friday we would have a spelling test of twenty words, and anyone who got less than eighteen correct was caned. I had never experienced corporal punishment before in my fluffy little bubble, and this cruelty made me a total shivering wreck. Thankfully, English was always my best subject and spelling was not a problem, so I was not personally targeted by this man. But to see my classmates ridiculed, having to stand up and be caned, completely traumatised me. It got to the stage that one Friday morning I fell to my knees and begged my mum not to send me to school. She acted immediately, thank goodness, and I did not return to that class – or indeed the junior school – at all.

It was arranged that I would change school and for the last junior year I was sent to a church school. It was quite a distance away from home, but the walk to get there by a little stream and up a hill, where wild flowers grew and birds sang, was so lovely. In modern times this walk would not have been safe, and for the first few weeks at my new school Mum would walk with me, but what a different life it became.

There were only three classes in the new school, and therefore eighteen children in my class year, which I found much easier to handle. The children were amazed because I could already do 'joined-up' writing, whilst they were still printing, and for the first time in my life I was proud of something. There were ten girls and eight boys. One boy had suffered polio when he was about five and I felt sorry for him as he, too, was bullied because he spoke slowly and walked with difficulty.

The wonderful headmaster, Mr Pitty, who was also our teacher, took us for nature walks, encouraged me to play the recorder and was wonderful in explaining things. It was the happiest year I had ever spent at school. His attitude made me feel that I could be involved, and there was no fear in asking him questions or being ridiculed. His wife included me in an embroidery class and I won first prize for a cushion-cover, which was amazing! Trivialities in the modern day and age, but they meant so much to me at a very difficult age.

When the eleven-plus loomed this was another problem. With the church school being so small, there was only one place at local grammar schools for a girl and one place for a boy. I somehow got onto the 'border-line' and had to re-sit the examination along with another girl in my class, and she came out two points higher and therefore got the coveted place. Actually this was a good thing, as I would never have coped with a bus journey to school on my own. I was blissfully unaware of my locality apart from the bus which took us to Manchester for shopping days, when I would be kept off school and have to take a note in the following day to say I had been unwell. Mum must have been a very good letter-writer – I wonder if school believed it all?

This 'failure' of the eleven-plus meant I had to return to my original school for the senior years, which was hard for me. Thankfully, I still had some friends there from before, and as it was now an 'all girls' school I hoped life would be better.

However, letters flew fast and furious from my mum to the school over the next few years. I was not to be involved in gym, netball or games. Gran complained about the sewing class as I was not doing things 'right', which infuriated the teacher, who made me unpick everything Gran had made me do at home. I was not to wear one of the school 'caps', which was a red jockey-cap with the school badge on, which Mum and Gran considered dreadful: instead I was given a navy-blue beret (which other girls found funny). But the worst was the domestic science class. We were given a list of ingredients each week for the following week's cookery class, but Mum and Gran adamantly refused to adhere to this. I understand it was probably because of my poor appetite, but it was so humiliating and embarrassing to be the 'odd one out' yet again. On the week where we were to take a piece of steak to cook, I was given an egg to take and just boiled that. I cannot describe the resulting bullying and intimidation I got from both the other girls and the cookery teacher every week thereafter. I did, however, learn how to iron handkerchiefs correctly and wash up! How I hated school, and was so unhappy.

Things did not improve either by the time I was twelve years old. By that time my teeth were beginning to decay due, probably, to the sugar 'butties' my mum insisted on feeding me, and of course not only did I never own a toothbrush but I never visited a dentist. I guess Mum thought she was being kind not putting me through her experience, but had she only known it she made life far worse for me. Things at school in the fifties were nowhere near as stringent as they are now, and I am sure this could not happen with the strategies in place today. Because of my dental problems I had many days off school with toothache, earache and badly swollen cheeks, but again this was never picked up on by the authorities and I have no recollection of Miss Bissett-Smith coming to our house at that time. She may have done, but if so it was never when I was at home.

I will not dwell on 'personal' items around the ages of thirteen and fourteen, and suffice to say that as no explanations of 'growing up' were given to me I went through some very traumatic experiences. The worst was that no essential 'items' were bought for me at all and I knew nothing of how my friends coped with 'growing up'. I learnt a few things from other girls of course – not always correct – but at least I realised I was not quite such an 'oddball' and that things which happened were 'normal'. However, when other girls of thirteen and fourteen were starting to talk about boys, I was still hurtling home at every conceivable moment to shut myself in our back room and play my imaginary games. I was not maturing in the right way – or indeed at all. Music did raise its head for me at that time though, and I loved the Sixties music on the radio and started recording on Dad's tape recorder, much to the disgust of Mum and Gran, who only liked 'Music While You Work' etc. From a very early age I had loved some of Dad's classical music – Bizet's *Carmen* for instance and music from *Midsummer Night's Dream* and ballet music, but Mum and Gran were not over-keen. However music has been the food of life for me from very early on – all sorts of music, and after I went to see *South Pacific* at the cinema with Mum I was also hooked on the musicals. What a different world I saw on the screen – full of love, romance, beautiful scenery, music and singing.

At the age of fourteen we were to be placed in different class groups: some girls to follow commercial subjects and others to follow science. Because my English was good I was placed in the commercial stream, and the first time I saw an ancient Olivetti typewriter that was it! Within a couple of weeks I was already building up touch-typing speed, and when the class did a 'demonstration' of typing to music I was not allowed to join in because I typed too fast! I had, at least, found my forté in life. I also began to learn shorthand, but due to catching chickenpox I was very ill for weeks and therefore way behind the other pupils when I returned, but at least my teacher could see some talent in me, somewhere. Mum was very generous at this time, as she purchased a portable typewriter for me, which came in very useful for practice. I wore that machine out, but have always loved keyboarding skills throughout my life.

In those days we left school at fifteen, and I could not wait. It had been suggested I go on to college to continue the commercial course, and Mum and Gran did agree to this. Still, the final humiliation at school still awaited me. Shortly before the leaving day my class was lined up outside the school hall, and one by one we were taken to see the school dentist! Humiliation and fear arose in me and quite rightly too. In front of all my classmates when my turn came round he said he had never seen such a state as my mouth was in for a fifteen-year-old girl, and wanted to know why I hadn't done something about it! Obviously I was in no fit state to say anything to him – how would any of these people realise what my home life was like or that I had no say in anything! He tut-tutted and groaned and then the female attendant said if I didn't get myself sorted out I would never get a job, looking like that! Talk about adding insult to injury. I did not tell Mum and Gran what had happened when I went home, but swallowed down the pain and distress as they would not have understood at all, and it would probably have meant more horrible letters being sent to school. I was far too immature and downtrodden to have the ability to do anything about it.

And so, at fifteen, I left school for good. How wonderful it was to walk out of those gates for the last time. College awaited the following September, but I didn't even have the ability to imagine how it would be. Still, there were the summer months to come when I could play my own games and be left alone before I had to deal with it ...

CHAPTER 3

Changes

———

Only a few months before leaving school at the age of fifteen we had moved house, which, looking back, was probably the first time I experienced a little bit of independence. The move was to a small hilltop village called Mottram on the edge of the Peak District, and very rural. From the front bay windows of the new house there was nothing but fields as far as the eye could see, haymaking in the late summer and autumn, rabbits in the fields, and beautiful seasonal changes throughout the year. I loved it from the start, and it had an indoor bathroom and toilet (hurrah). As the semi-detached house was high above the road (fourteen steps up to the front door) it meant there was a large expanse of sky at the front, giving fabulous sunsets and a wide view from left to right over the fields and hills.

It was sad to leave the only house I could remember, but this was something of an adventure in an otherwise very static existence at the age of fourteen and a half. Having had a 75 ft garden at our previous house, the new property had a smaller plot at the back and quite a good frontage. For some reason I took instant delight in turning it from a weed-locked mess into something resembling a proper garden ready for plants. I worked hard, digging and turning the soil over (although Mum and Gran were not too happy, as this should not be 'ladies' work), but gosh did I find it therapeutic.

Dad wasn't too happy about the move, as from our old house, which fronted a main road, he only had to catch a bus straight into Manchester where he worked in Lewis's Department Store. Now, however, he had a fairly long commute with a long walk to the nearest station and a steep hill to navigate on the journey home, after a long physical hard-working day. Knowing the situation with our two matriarchs, I doubt if he had much say in the matter of moving house – if any. It would be a done deal when they made their minds up, and in later years I believe I discovered the reason behind this move ...

Having a few months left at senior school this event meant I had to catch a bus to school for the final months before leaving. There was almost a mile walk to the bus stop in the centre of the village, but it was the first time I had gone *anywhere* on my own – even only three miles into Hyde! It thus opened some new experiences and ideas, as regular travelling companions at the bus stop (usually an elderly lady and a young woman) began talking to me and I started to realise how nice it was to hold conversations with other people. Goodness knows what we talked about, as I had little if any life experience, but I guess it was just about school or what they were doing. Anyway, travelling this way gave me the time and freedom to think about things in general by watching how others acted – 'people watching', in fact. It was very different to what I had been used to!

Being in a rural home, my closest friends Lynne and Ann visited sometimes over the next year or so, but of course as we finished school they both went into jobs and I commenced college, so our paths did not cross again for some time. Lynne turned up a couple of times and we had a lovely country walk together, but she told me in later years she never felt 'welcome'. She felt that visiting was intrusive. We met up again nine years later by accident and have kept in touch ever since.

Ann and I had managed to join a tennis club in Mottram for a few months, but once again after leaving school her life took a different path and it was another six years before she visited me briefly, and then it took forty-seven years before I traced her again. We immediately took up our friendship, despite the missing years, which is lovely.

The summer months after leaving school were idyllic, and then as September loomed many doubts and fears reared their heads. How on earth would I cope? I had plenty of time to think about the matter and consider it was around this time that other questions began to surface in my mind. For instance, we had a lovely bureau in our dining room which had a centre cupboard. That cupboard was always kept firmly locked and should I ever have reason (which wasn't often) to go into the bureau for, say, a pen or some paper, a very careful eye was kept on me. Of course, I asked what was in there, but never got an answer.

I also began to realise how very different I looked from my parents, whereas my friends all had some sort of familiar feature to theirs. I was much taller, slim, and bore no resemblance to them whatsoever in either looks or character. Mum and Gran always tried very hard to mould me into a copy of themselves, but it was never going to happen. I was completely different but understood they were not a 'birth' family, and that was the reason. It did make life difficult many times, but I had great respect for them and would always do exactly what they told me to. Nothing else was acceptable, as I could not think for myself at all, never having had the opportunity.

Something must have happened at one point when I was around fourteen or fifteen, as I unexpectedly discovered a letter on my little bedroom table from my mum. It simply stated that it was the 'only way' she could communicate with me as I was becoming rude and cheeky – that sort of tone. I was told I had to think very carefully about my attitude and be much more respectful. Goodness knows what brought this on, as I could never say boo to a goose, and I certainly would never have knowingly crossed either of them! I was upset about this

With Mum and Dad at Mottram and our neighbour's little dog "Whisky",
aged 15.

for a long time but it was never mentioned or discussed and simply served to make me withdraw even more into myself. Why didn't they feel we could hold a discussion? I shall never know.

College was the window into the future for me. The first day was difficult because of my insecurity and shyness, but thankfully one of the girls I knew from another class in school started on the same day, and she was also a fairly shy girl. We got on well, and managed to cope with the first few days of college, when we felt like fish out of water. Boys were a problem for both of us as well – Elisabeth because of her shyness and me because of my backward attitude and appearance. I had been 'allowed' to have my plaits cut off (at age fifteen?) and now wore my hair shorter. Having been allowed glasses with a proper frame they were also improved, but the teeth and my gangly gaunt figure did not give me any confidence whatsoever.

I had a teacher at college who became my lifeline. The teachers there treated us so differently than at school. We were considered young adults and for the first time in my life I felt as if someone older was talking to me as a person, not a 'to be hidden' child. I had found my forté in the work, which I loved, and went from strength to strength in all commercial subjects. Miss D., the teacher with whom we had most lessons, was an inspiration for me and although she never enquired about my home life she obviously had an idea that there were a few difficulties. I enjoyed learning for the first time ever, and could not wait to arrive at college every morning. Lunch was taken in the cafeteria, and then I would go next door (the library and college shared the same building) into the reference library where I took copious notes in shorthand about local history, and then in an evening I would happily type up the notes at home on the portable typewriter, which was fabulous practice for both skills. Learning about the local areas also inspired my love of archaeology and history, which continued throughout the rest of my life. At least it was taking me away from the 'pretend' world a little, although not completely.

Miss D. had to undergo having all her teeth removed towards the end of the first college year, and I am certain that she used this situation to attempt to help me, who by this time was in a dreadful dental state, to put it mildly. She did it with such tact and diplomacy that it gave me the courage to approach my dad and tell him how I felt, which really was indescribable. I think he was glad I had at last realised the need to sort it out. Of course I never knew what had gone on behind my back between Mum, Gran and Dad, but I suspect he had said plenty which had fallen on deaf ears regarding this situation. After breaking up from college, he accompanied me to a local dentist and I underwent the removal of every single tooth. I am not dwelling on this, as for six weeks (in those days) there were no replacements, but by the time college recommenced in September I had a completely new appearance, could close my mouth properly, and had a bit more confidence in myself! At least now I did not mind glancing in the mirror, with complete thanks to Miss D.'s care and help, who was delighted when we met up again.

Recommencement of college had been quite an item at home. As I did so well, passing around twelve examinations in the first year, Miss D. sent my parents a letter requesting that I be allowed to attend full-time college for a second year, as she felt it would be a good opportunity for me. Mum and Gran were against this, as they thought I should now get a job – in later life I understood why, as they wished me to earn some money, but at the time I did not. For once, however, Dad got his way. He insisted I return and continue my education as he strongly felt girls should have a career to strengthen their lives, as should they ever be left alone with a family to support they would be able to do so with a skill. He won his case after considerable argument, and I happily returned. In the two years at college I passed twenty-eight examinations, some with distinction, and when I left at the age of seventeen went straight into a good job, thanks to my dad.

It was the advent of college and being treated so differently that my thought processes began to change. Seeing how other girls acted, the freedom they had, their relationships with their parents (although teenage girls can find that difficult) and the fact I spent most of my time at home still 'playing' imaginary games showed me how insular I was. The surrounding countryside in Mottram opened my eyes to the beauty outside, whereas I still inhabited my own drab little world. Realisation began to dawn on me that I was almost a young adult, not a child anymore, although the rules at home never changed. I certainly did not feel anywhere near being an adult, although at college I was made to feel worthy, which pushed me to do my very best. I spent a lot of time alone at home. Apart from

Aged 17 – too thin!

watching 'suitable' television programmes, the majority of my time was spent in the dining room playing those silly games by myself whilst listening to *Top of the Pops* on the radio and brilliant Sixties music. Most of my friends went out in evenings to the local hall, where they jived and rock 'n rolled etc., and they would come to college the next day relating their adventures and who they 'fancied'. That was an alien world to me, and one I would never have been allowed to join.

Never having been given any information about the 'birds and bees', I was completely unaware of anything relating to the opposite sex, and to be honest it didn't interest me, as I knew how Mum and Gran felt about men and boys. I did have teenage 'crushes' on various male pop stars, but didn't really understand what that was all about!

Not having the tiniest bit of a rebellious nature, which perhaps was banished from me very early on, I was easy prey to be dominated and bossed around. I began to wonder about many things which were taboo. What was in that locked section of the bureau, for instance? Were there papers in there relating to me? Perhaps not; probably just private papers of the household. Adoption was better understood by me now, and occasionally I did wonder just what could have happened to me. Where was my birth mother? Who was she? Did she ever think about me – particularly on my birthday? Who was my father? That question did not concern me as much as my birth mother, as I already had the most wonderful Dad on earth. Lots of little questions would claim my attention as I looked around the other girls in my class at college – one in particular, who became pregnant at the age of fifteen. Is that what happened to my birth mother? It was no use asking any questions as the 'situation' simply did not exist in the minds of Mum and Gran, and I had no wish to bring down their fury upon my head by trying.

When we first moved house, Mum and Gran began to attend the local congregational church, and of course I went with them. They had often 'tried out' various churches when we lived in Hyde, but for some unknown reason these times did not last long and a new church would be visited. It was the same with the Mothers' Union, which didn't last long. Mum and Gran simply did not seem to like people. I discovered a few nice young people at this congregational church, and when, as expected, Mum and Gran filtered out of their visits, I continued to go and actually was given a Sunday school class of five-year olds for a short time. What a responsibility, but it was lovely. There was also a youth group, which Mum and Gran thought was suitable, as it appertained to church, and for a few months I enjoyed the company of these lovely young people.

I was almost seventeen at this time and due to leave college to commence work, when a catastrophic event occurred which split me from even the church group.

I was asked if I would like to accompany them – a group of around fourteen young people, boys and girls, to travel up to the vicar's house at Charlesworth, which was around five miles away. Three cars would be going and the group had been asked if they would 'babysit' the vicar's two young children on New Year's Eve whilst the vicar and his wife visited family. This seemed a lovely idea and was approved by my matriarchs, unbelievably!

I was duly picked up from the front door and three cars made the short journey. It was such a lovely evening – no alcohol of course. Games such as Monopoly (which I had never seen or played before), The New Seekers' music playing all evening, soft drinks, snacks, a lot of laughter and completely innocent fun. What I had not realised is that the vicar and his wife would not return until almost 1 a.m. By that time the church group were singing religious songs, pop songs and simply sitting round in a circle sharing laughter and chatting. We duly set off back home just after 1 a.m. and when we pulled up at my home there on the doorstep were Mum and Gran – absolutely furious. They shouted across the road immediately about how worried they were, what time was this, we could have had an accident and ended up in the river etc. etc. They were livid. (It would never have occurred to me to be so cheeky as to use the vicar's telephone, as of course there were no mobiles in those days). I got out of the car as quickly as I could and ran in – so humiliated and upset to be shown up in this way. Dad tried to be the peace-maker, but needless to say I did not attend the group any more as I was so ashamed, and neither did I ever receive any further invitations.

Whilst I had been at the congregational church, one friend I had made there had asked me to go with her to a dancing school in Hyde, three miles away. This was considered suitable of course, as it was ballroom dancing, so we went together on the bus for the first lesson. My friend did not care for it at all, but I was hooked, and so for the next four years I regularly attended – firstly on Saturdays and then on Tuesday evenings as well. In the later years when we had a family car Mum and Dad would take me there then meet me later on. I was not allowed to go alone – even when I was almost twenty! However, I loved every moment of it and made some nice friends, usually dancing with the teacher or another girl. There were one or two boys but they were definitely in the minority and already with a partner, so obviously Mum and Gran considered it 'safe'. There was one boy, who was fourteen – three years my junior – and we partnered each other for a couple of years as the steps just seemed to 'gel' between us and that was wonderful. He stopped coming to the classes when he left school, but Strictly would have been proud of us (except we didn't do acrobatics!). I actually passed some dancing exams and received medals for Ballroom and Latin American. It was the one thing in my late teens which I thoroughly enjoyed. However, life was such an enigma – on the one hand I was kept a child and on the other had to be a 'responsible' adult.

Aged 18 with Gran at Rhos-on-Sea.

It seemed to be taken for granted that I knew everything I needed, but in fact I did not, and had neither the tenacity or courage to go against Mum and Gran's wishes.

And so the year progressed, and just before leaving college at the end of my second year it was time to find a job. Without saying, Mum and Gran were very involved in this, and it was arranged on my behalf to have an interview with the solicitor who had done the house conveyancing for them when we moved from Hyde. He was called Mr O. and worked in a small brick-built office near to Hyde Post Office and Fire Station. His firm was downstairs, and another firm of solicitors worked from the upstairs floor.

Mum accompanied me to my interview – I doubt if I would have known or had the courage to say anything in any event! I took all my exam certificates with me, and he seemed to be very pleased and offered me a job on the spot as his secretary. Wow! That had all happened without my having to speak at all! I was never asked how I felt about it, but although it seemed wonderful it was going to be an eye-opener for me without any doubt, and would take some courage and a lot of learning in order to cope. Could I do that?

Attired in a lovely navy-blue suit bought especially for my new career, I was made very welcome by the three girls who were also employed at the office. There was a clerk, an office junior (yes, I ranked above her; weird!), another secretary who worked for the clerk and a secretary from the firm upstairs, who actually became a lifelong friend. The clerk, Mrs B., swore like a trooper, which was something very new to me, but I learnt to laugh about it and she was very helpful in teaching me the ropes. Mr O. himself trained me in legal matters as he was a man of the 'old school', and everything had to be 100% precise. If something was not right it was done again – and again if necessary. I suspect previous secretaries had found this too hard, but I really liked it as I am a perfectionist by nature, and his training was the best it could have been.

He was also rather eccentric in some ways. He knew to the last paper clip how many were in his desk tray, and each night would leave little notes on the typewriters for us to find in the morning, pointing out various things he wished to be put right in the office. He *never* threw a used envelope away and as a result all four walls of his office were stacked high with them, which he used as scrap paper. Mr O. was a nice person though, and would frequently take off in his car to the north of Scotland if an albatross or rare bird was seen, as he was an avid bird watcher.

I have never been able to understand why Mum and Gran had such odd and contradictory ideas about me. They kept me in childhood just as long as they could, protected and shielded me from the outside world, and then at the tender age of seventeen gave me the great responsibility of driving a vehicle! I had never even been in a car apart from one visit we had from an uncle and aunt who had a Ford, and the uncle had taken me a ride round the block whilst parking his car. I had never known anything about the workings of a car, the foot pedals or anything relating to road procedure at all. In my childhood holidays to Southport, Wales or (what seemed the end of the earth to me – Littlehampton on the south coast), we had used bus or train. Because I was so ignorant about how cars worked my dad, bless him, made me a mock setup of the foot pedals out of wood to practice on at home, but to be honest that didn't help much as they did not move!

On my actual seventeenth birthday I walked out of college and my new driving instructor was waiting for me in a lovely lemon and white Triumph Herald. Mum and Gran had decided it would be nice for the family to have a car, and I was the obvious choice to take the responsibility for driving it and be the first to pass the test. I would then be able to teach Dad and Mum, in that order. There wasn't really a lot to teach either of them, as both had driven before the war, although neither had taken a driving test as it did not exist in those pre-war days. I have to admit my dad was not very keen at all because of the expense of running a car, but of course he did not have a say in the matter.

Thankfully I had a great driving instructor, and the first time I got into a car behind the driving wheel is something I have never forgotten. Power! I loved it, but it took me quite a long time and many hours of practice to actually realise how the Highway Code and actual road procedure worked. Thankfully there were not as many cars on the road back then as there are now, but what a world it opened to me. A kind neighbour sat with me several times whilst I practised driving, and then one day I had a sort of 'enlightenment' and everything dropped into place. I was driving properly, and enjoying it. I have loved it all my life.

Independence, enjoyment and freedom. I passed my test six months later on 13 August, and on the day a Morris Minor was purchased by Mum and Gran I had the responsibility of it. Our driveway at home was a nightmare: there was no dropped kerb and the drive itself was very steep indeed. I had to bump the car up the kerb and then up another sharp edge onto the drive, which was grass, with only two rows of paving stones up to the top for the wheels to grip. In the winter it was awful, quite severe with ice and snow-drifts because we lived so near to the open moors. I guess it taught me steadfastness and determination, as I was the only one who could manoeuvre this driveway, but it also frightened me and frequently I would have a private cry at the pressure.

At least for a couple of years, from seventeen to nineteen, I had a job I really enjoyed and loved learning about conveyancing, probate and wills; could drive a car, which meant driving to lovely places on Sunday taking Mum, Dad and Gran of course; looked forward to the dancing, which spilled over onto two evenings a week by then as well as Saturdays, and at least life seemed quite full and 'out in the world'. But, of course, it wasn't.

CHAPTER 4

A New Life

Driving certainly opened a whole new world to me and I loved every moment. In a way it was freedom, although most of the trips I made (apart from three miles to work when I was allowed to take the car), were to take Mum, Dad and Gran out on a Sunday. With two back-seat drivers who were always telling me I was driving too fast because they couldn't see the scenery properly it was not easy, but we went to many places of interest: the seaside of course, and even down to the south coast of England to Littlehampton on holiday. I was teaching my dad to drive at that point so we were able to each have a break on what seemed such a long journey back in 1965 and 1966, as most roads were 'A' roads, but I remember well the infant M1, which had very little traffic on it back then!

There was one incident when I was around eighteen which has stuck in my mind ever since. Had I known then what I know now, my life would have been completely turned around – and so would the lives of a lot of other people too! However, I would never have been forgiven.

During the early years of World War II Dad was sent to a training camp at Saighton near Chester, and on one of our day trips to Chester he mentioned he would like to revisit the site just for interest. I remember well the major fuss this caused with Mum and Gran – they did their best to dissuade him but he stuck firm. I was completely innocent and unaware of their reasons, but of course never questioned anything in those days. We did not go into the village itself, which is a couple of

39

Visit to Saighton Camp, near Chester. Dad, Mum and Gran

miles from the centre of Chester, but we stopped outside the old camp which was still maintained and occupied in 1967. He obviously had many memories of that time, but of course the two ladies were absolutely disgusted. Dad took a photograph of me walking down the beautiful tree-lined lane outside the camp, and that picture has always stuck in my mind, despite my being completely oblivious of its potential meaning. I was wearing a 'Parisian pink' dress – but that photograph disappeared many moons ago.

Many lives apart from mine would have been very different if I had been told the truth at that time.

Coming up to the ages of nineteen and twenty were, in a way, quite an epoch for me. Not a particularly happy one at the beginning, but it led to a more independent and fulfilling life opening up.

From the age of fourteen I had belonged to a 'penfriend club' – meaning people wrote to each other from all over the world. This was not a dating site such as we hear about now, but was meant simply to make new friends. With the advent of mobile phones, Facebook and social media I guess penfriends have virtually died out as technology has increased and letter-writing is becoming rare. At one time I had over twenty penfriends – the postage would be prohibitive these days, but it wasn't too bad in the late 1960s. I wrote to people from New Zealand, Australia, America and of course all over England – young people like myself who simply liked writing (and typing in my case). Even now I am still in touch with one friend in Australia, one in New Zealand and a family in America whose daughter and I began writing to each other when she was eight and I was just nine!

By the time in question when I was nearing twenty, I was still enjoying the dancing and, of course, work, but I knew in my heart that my current job was not going anywhere. I took the unprecedented step of stating I was looking for another job – this time in Manchester, which was almost eight miles away. This statement did not go down too well at home, but Dad backed me up. I had been offered training for court reporting due to my fast typing and shorthand speeds, but Dad suggested I wait a couple of years – he knew I would not cope with travelling around the country on my own, even though I was nineteen, and he above anyone understood how unwordly I was. In effect I think he knew it would be dangerous for me to go down such a road at that particular time.

I knew wages and experience would be much better in Manchester and therefore I looked for an opening in Dad's newspapers. I soon found one and wrote a letter of application which resulted in an appointment for an interview. This was probably the first time in my life I had made a decision for myself. Now, bearing in mind I had never travelled alone into Manchester at that time (unbelievable though that may be), my mum insisted on accompanying me to that interview. I was totally embarrassed and dumfounded, but she would not be deterred and along she came – and into the interview room itself! The solicitor who interviewed me. Mr B., was obviously rather taken aback when 'my mother' walked into the office with me, (ostensibly to 'hold my hand'), but the production of my exam certificates and my telling him what legal experience I had up to that time resulted in my being offered the job after I was given a test. This new job would cover a bit more of the legal spectrum – it was a much bigger office and had opportunity for progress.

So the first day of the new job arrived. Never had I expected so much fuss over a bus ride into Manchester! Still, I obviously survived it and a new chapter opened. The office, however, brought a few difficulties. The other girls were much more streetwise and I simply didn't understand a lot of the banter that went on between them. I knew how 'green behind the ears' I was, which resulted in some of the women becoming rather bullying, and I realised very quickly that I was a figure of fun to them – someone out of the 'Ark'. My boss, however, Mr B., soon became a wonderful friend and I worked really hard, which he appreciated greatly. He loved my quick speeds at shorthand and typing, and we also utilised the new dictaphone system, which meant saving time. He trusted me and that meant a lot. When, two years later he took up a new post with the CWS. Legal Department he asked me to go there to continue working for him, and this I did.

This new job meant a big change in my life and in some ways I learnt more about the city around me, although I am sure the other office girls considered me a 'swot', as with me it was head down and churn out as much work as I could. I loved that work. The other secretaries met up socially – after work or to a night club, and of course I did not join in with these things. I had to go home, whatever happened. Actually, their type of social life would not have suited me, as I would have been most uncomfortable.

I loved working in the centre of Manchester – the bustle, history, shops and eclectic mixture of people were fantastic, although travelling by bus meant the journeys to and from work were long. In the end I decided to use the train service from Broadbottom, which only took twenty minutes but was a longer walk, involving a steep hill and a further walk in Manchester itself.

Possibly witnessing the lives of the new girls I was working with made me more aware of how few friends I had at that time. I put a posting in to the penfriend club and decided to take on more friends to try and boost my non-existent social life, despite them only being on paper. Several replies came and correspondence was commenced, which I thoroughly enjoyed. However, it did not take the place of 'actual' contact friendships, which I really missed. The 'pretend' world was still more real to me than reality.

I received one letter of reply from a prospective penfriend, Ian, who only lived around four miles away. This was a young man of twenty-eight, who had seen in my profile that I did ballroom dancing. He explained in his first letter that he did shift work and therefore it was difficult to have regular hours, and that he was too shy to socialise much. He would really like to learn dancing, but although he had attempted to go to a dancing school in Manchester he had not coped with it, as he did not have the confidence which was needed. I replied to him as I did to all the others at that time, some of whom lived in places as far away as Scotland and Cornwall. I soon realised that this young man was really nice and more shy even than myself, so in a way I guess I felt sorry for him. I told him about the dancing school I attended, which was local, very small and run by a nice married couple, and suggested he could try that, as it would be much more comfortable than a large school. This seemed to appeal to him, and he asked if he could

The first photograph I ever took of Ian, 1968.

accompany me one evening. Oh dear – that would not go down well with Mum and Gran!

They agreed (unbelievably) that he could accompany me, on the understanding that he would come to our house so everyone could meet him (and be approved, of course), and then if he came dancing with me at a later date he could come to my home and we would *both* be taken and met again afterwards. They weren't taking any chances! So, an arrangement was made for him to visit us, and on 13 August 1968 I first heard the chug-chug of his Lambretta scooter arriving on our driveway. Although I had seen a photograph of him, when I opened the front door and he came in I thought what a nice person he was. Very good looking.

It was a very awkward evening. We sat in the lounge with Mum, Dad and Gran, and Ian sat there stuttering and stumbling with nerves, kneading his trouser leg in his anxiety.

It was a very stunted conversation indeed, although he always answered when spoken to. He mentioned he had a stamp collection (ugh!), but my dad was very interested in that, and the evening culminated with an arrangement for him to return the following evening to show Dad his collection!

We continued to correspond, and after he had taken a holiday to visit his aunt in the south of England it was arranged he would come over one Thursday evening when he was on an early shift and go dancing with me. He was a complete bag of nerves, but I managed to propel him around the dance floor within the limits of his sense of rhythm; he could not relax in that strange environment. He came two or three times after that, and when we were taken back to my home he would stay for a cuppa before going home (no spirits or wine in our house of course – they were unknown!). And so we did get to grips with some conversation. His main loves in life were hiking and camping, and eventually in the early months of spring the following year, just as I turned twenty, he asked if I would like to go on a local day's walk with him. He was being very brave!

People would not believe the comments I had from Mum and Gran when I said I would like to accompany Ian on this walk, from Buxton to Tissington Gates, walking down beautiful Dovedale. They gave me dire warnings about not walking 'too far', pushing the fact I didn't really know this person etc. etc. and said that too much strenuous walking would not be good for me! But I still went. It was a lovely day: spring sunshine, beautiful scenery I had never witnessed before, really relaxing and enjoyable. We chatted amicably and shared a lovely picnic near Dovestones, and then when we returned to Buxton for the train back home we went into a café for a meal. Ian could not believe me at all. A bowl of soup was all I had – that was a meal for me. He tucked into a large mixed grill, but at that point I still could not eat such meals. I did, however, manage a sweet that day, which was a first – the fresh air had obviously sharpened my appetite to a certain extent! It goes without saying that I was very thin indeed.

After that first date we went to the pictures, and he visited me at home on various occasions. We would spend time together in the dining room playing cards – all sorts of card games, quite innocent with no sign of romance whatsoever. Still, the companionship we had was lovely, as he was such a nice young man – in fact there was nothing one couldn't like about him.

Mum, Gran and even Dad were not too sure. Ian was eight years my senior, and I guess they were concerned about my total inexperience around boys or men – Dad being the only man I had ever really talked to apart from the two solicitors I had worked for. However, Ian was the perfect companion for me. He was shy, but the most truthful, honest, considerate and understanding person I had ever met. He was the perfect partner for me, as with my inexperience I did not feel in any way threatened or under pressure from him. He was as inexperienced with women as I was with men. An only child, like myself, but his mother had made him fiercely independent and he really, I guess, was something of a 'loner' in many respects. It was probably the fact that I had actually met someone shyer than myself which brought out my protective instincts, and we got on very well right from the start.

As I was now working in Manchester and Ian worked at the Royal Mail Head Office in Manchester, he would often meet me for lunch before going onto a late shift, and whenever possible, which was most weekend Sundays, we would either go for a walk, or in bad weather simply go to see a film or play cards at home. It was that simple. Nothing to set the world on fire, but it suited us both. Eventually after a few months I was invited to his parents' house for tea. The first words his mum said to me were 'I never thought he was going to bring a girl home!' By that time he was twenty-eight! What lovely people his parents were. His mum, a Yorkshire lass, was very straightforward, and his dad was a facsimile of Ian – so shy and quiet. They were greatly involved in the local church, and his mum went swimming three times a week right up until her late eighties. She was a really solid, healthy woman, always active and busy with a house full of friends and neighbours all the time. It was such a different atmosphere from my own home, and I grew to love going there.

Ian and I suited each other well. Our companionship was always amiable and pleasant, we enjoyed the same interests, and those first few months were, for me, some of the happiest I had ever known with the freedom to get out and about, visit places and enjoy the company of a very nice person. I was never allowed to ride pillion on Ian's scooter, so all our trips out were by bus or train, unless I was allowed the use of the car, which was infrequent. We were not really trusted.

Of course things had to come to a head at some point, and seven months later on Christmas Eve, which was Ian's birthday, he took me for a meal in the centre of Manchester; a brand-new experience for me! I still was not eating properly but had improved slightly, and that was a lovely evening. It suddenly occurred to me whether a 'big question' was going to be asked, and I got rather scared. It never happened, but the walk home from the station up the hill to my home that evening was never to be forgotten. It started to snow, and we could hear the church bells in Mottram ringing out Christmas carols. It was the sort of evening which should have been recorded for posterity; it was so beautiful, with the ice sparkling on the hedges in the darkness and snow softly falling. We were both so introverted in our ways that neither of us had either the courage or words to say how romantic it could be, but looking back I am sure that is what we both felt.

It was in January that Ian actually 'spoke'. Really, he had no choice! We were looking at the newspaper trying to decide which film we should go to see, when he suddenly suggested that we could take a week's holiday together in Oban and do some hill walking. Oh dear, that really put me on the spot. I tried to tactfully explain that I did not think my mum and gran would like that one little bit, regardless of how 'innocent' it might be. Scotland might have as well have been Australia for me, as I had not travelled far, and I still felt I had to get Mum and Gran's permission to agree to this trip. Ridiculous really, but that is how it was.

Ian therefore suddenly stuttered out 'Will you marry me, then?' I guess he thought being engaged would help, not yet knowing the might of my matriarchs' power! However, I stuttered back a quick 'yes', and he promptly disappeared upstairs to the bathroom to be alone after finding the courage for such a huge event! So, we were engaged. Yes – me – engaged! That was beyond the wildest dream I had ever dared to dream, as I had always thought myself too ugly and stupid, and although it was not the most romantic of proposals I was so very happy, as I thought a lot of Ian and probably knew in my heart I would never have the opportunity to meet such another lovely man to share my life with, and whom I trusted one hundred percent. Still, now there was the difficulty of telling my parents!

When I did pluck up the courage to advise Mum and Gran of the situation, they just said 'Oh, we're not surprised', and that was it. End of subject. No congratulations. I was turning twenty-one in the February, so this became a joint engagement and twenty-first party. However, we were snowed in on the actual date so the few people Mum and Gran had invited couldn't get to us – Ian did though – he left his scooter six miles away and hiked the rest of the way to be with me on that date. We had the celebration the following week, and the trip to Oban was planned.

That was a holiday to remember, and the first time I had ever been away from home. I know it was definitely frowned upon, but we were sensible people and stayed at a B & B in Oban – in separate rooms. One problem had been the

Engagement Day and my 21st birthday, 16th February 1969.

procurement of trousers for me to wear, as mountain walking was tough and suitable attire was essential. Had I bought trousers ('ladies never wore trousers'), they would have promptly been burnt or thrown out by Mum and Gran, so we deceitfully purchased two pairs for me one lunchtime in Manchester and Ian took them home and put them in *his* case. I spent that week's holiday terrified Mum and Gran would pop round a corner or a rock and see me wearing them; their power was so strong! Of course it couldn't happen, as Oban was so far away, but I felt guilty the whole time! This seems to be so silly seventy-odd years later, and I realise frequently how different and happier a time it could have been.

It was a good week, although very strenuous for me, and on the train home I actually burst into tears. Ian could not understand this, but it was because I was going back home.

Losing the freedom I had experienced for the first time in my life, going back to be dominated and ruled once more.

The threads of life were picked up again, and we decided to book our wedding for one and a half years later, in June 1970. When we got engaged I had told Ian that I was adopted, but his only reaction was, 'You are you – there's no such thing as an illegitimate child; only illegitimate parents.' The information that I gave to him created huge repercussions the following year!

It felt as if our wedding day would never arrive, but we started to save up and managed to put a deposit on a little town house, which was in a new estate being built in Denton, near Manchester – around four miles from Mum, Dad and Gran. We put the deposit down on a grass plot, and then watched our new home being built. It was completed just three months before our wedding, but we were never allowed to be in there on our own – no way! When it came to measuring and planning we were *always* accompanied. As I have said before, Ian understood the situation and never added to it by going against my family, for which I was grateful.

Having attended the necessary interview with the local vicar when booking our wedding, I arrived home a week or so later and discovered a brown envelope addressed to Ian and I. Upon opening this it had the clarification of the wedding details and a small booklet 'About Married Life' etc. As soon as I took this out of the envelope Gran snatched it and condemned it to the back of the fire. 'Disgusting,' they both said. When I told Ian about this it was the only time in the thirty-six years we were to be together that I saw him really angry. Thankfully for me, he did not pursue the matter with them.

We were to marry on the 6th of June 1970 – D-Day, as my dad pointed out, but for me it was D-Day in more ways than one. It would mean at last living my own life and becoming half of a partnership where we two alone would decide things. No – that was in dreamland of course!

Three weeks before our wedding Mum cornered me in the dining room with a very red face, and whispered (it couldn't be said out loud, of course), 'Do you want me to tell Ian?' I didn't know what she meant, so she said, 'You know – about you being adopted.' Of course I had told Ian when we became engaged, so I explained this to her and she raged at me, almost screaming that it was not up to me to tell him, that *she* was the one who should have done this, and that it was nothing to do with me! I was very upset, but actually it made me even more curious to know how and why on earth Mum and Gran had taken me on – what did they know, and what was such a huge secret? Looking back now after fifty years, I suspect in their way it was to protect me, for illegitimacy was a real stigma in the post-war years right up into the 1970s, and perhaps they did not want me to be the butt of bullies or people who would have considered it a dreadful thing. I shall never know and at the time I did believe I had been adopted legally.

Our wedding was not a large affair. Mum and Gran marched me to C & A in Manchester and I bought the first wedding dress I saw off the peg for £25, the reception was organised by Ian's mother in their church hall, my wedding invitations were sent out by Mum and Gran to people they thought suitable, without reference to myself, and the flowers and wedding cake were made for us by two lovely ladies at Ian's mum's church. Dad did ask me if I had any friends I should like to invite, but I had lost touch with most of my previous schoolfriends. I did ask the girls I worked with if they would like to come to the church, but because they were not invited to a 'proper' evening no one turned up. Looking back at the group photograph outside the church the majority of the people were friends of Mum and Gran – Ian's side only had around ten people there.

It goes without saying I did my own hair and had no makeup or fancy nails. It might sound very sparse compared with the huge pageants of today, but it was one of the happiest days of my life. The church bells rang out for us, it was a sizzling hot June day and it was almost like a dream – I could not believe it was happening. None of my 'friends' were present except for my two Matrons of Honour – Kathleen, whom I had stayed friendly with from working for Mr O., and Brenda, who was the daughter of family friends and someone I really loved.

It all went off very well indeed and we left after the wedding lunch, as we were driving up to Bowness on Windermere in the Lake District for our honeymoon. Collecting the lovely bright brand-new red Vauxhall Viva caused a little difficulty as I had taken out the insurance as driver in my maiden name but was picking it up in my new married name. Ian did not have a licence to drive a car – just his scooter, so I drove us everywhere we went. We had a wonderful time, walking, visiting places, driving around without anyone interfering: it was a heatwave and the hydrangeas, roses and flowering shrubs were showing off their beauty magnificently. It was complete freedom for me and we were so happy. At the end of the week we returned for the first time to our own little home. It was simply magical. Mum and Gran had stood our wedding cards around the lounge, and it looked so beautiful. So began a new era – and a new life. Little did I know what the forthcoming years would unfold for me.

6th June 1970 "D-Day".

CHAPTER 5

Questions

———

I had entered a new kingdom. Our 'House O' Dreams' was exactly that. Setting up our first home together was so wonderful and for the first time I felt freedom to lead life as I wished – well, nearly! We were so happy and I still couldn't believe this was 'ours'.

I taught myself to bake, sew and do all sorts of things to make our meagre incomes cover what was needed. We had not bought much furniture; just taken my dad's advice to buy good carpets, to which we added what we could afford. Ian's parents had given us a refrigerator (their old one) which was very useful, and Gran had made curtains for our large dining room and lounge picture windows. Dad soon built us some kitchen units he had managed to salvage from Lewis's, and Mum had laid in a stock of table-cloths, tea towels etc. We also received some lovely wedding gifts, and I had collected little bits and pieces in my 'bottom drawer' over the one and a half years we were engaged.

The tiny plots at the back and front of our new house were difficult to turn into gardens due to rubbish and bricks the builders had covered over, but Ian soon sorted those out and installed neat lawns and flower borders. He was such a perfectionist – it wouldn't have surprised me if I had discovered him ironing the grass! I found it all so exciting and was thrilled with my new home despite not having a washing machine, television or such things.

The first year seemed to fly by with settling into our new

On honeymoon in Bowness, Windermere, June 1970.

life. Dad was the driver now, having passed his test, so Mum
and Gran would visit unannounced and probably at weekends.
I learnt to take no notice of what other people thought we
should or should not change around in the house. Some of it
was good advice, for which I was grateful, but it was very easy
to upset the applecart!

We managed to purchase a little old red and black Austin
A40 shortly after our first wedding anniversary and took our
first holiday, which was quite an experience for me! Ian had
always loved camping and that was all we could afford to do.
He had a two-man scout tent (no sewn-in groundsheet) and
some basic equipment, so we loaded up the little car and drove
up the west, along the north and back down the east coasts of
Scotland. Ian had not yet passed his driving test and only held

a provisional licence, but we were able to share the driving between us as I held a full licence. We pitched the little tent at the various campsites en route and cooked by means of a pressure cooker, although I still didn't eat very much. This being my first experience of camping, and the fact it rained every day except two in the fortnight, meant it was not a fabulous time.

Still, we were happy, did lots of walking, and it was my first visit to Scotland, which I grew to love. Ian was an avid hill and mountain walker, so he climbed Cairngorm whilst we were in Scotland whilst I sat by the loch below getting eaten by black flies! On our honeymoon in the Lake District I had climbed Helvellyn with him, but have to admit Striding Edge had rather put me off mountains considerably!

For much of our first married year and now having survived the holiday, during which I had plenty of time to think about things, I couldn't help trying to sort out the rigmarole in my head regarding my origins. At that time I was really mixed up, and had realised I could not have been legally adopted. Working in a legal office it had become clear that having my original birth certificate meant that I was not adopted after all, so must have been long-term fostered!

I had been handed a shortened version of my birth certificate for the first time by Mum just before Ian and I married. There was a little note attached to the top corner by a safety pin which said 'adopted' and had the family name on it. This was in Mum's handwriting. The certificate itself, however, showed my original birth surname of 'Ashton'. In 1970, upon marriage, it was not a requirement to produce a birth certificate as it would be in modern times, and it did not occur to me even then that perhaps I should have married with my original birth surname. I used the only surname I had ever known throughout my childhood and for some time in later years I did wonder if the marriage was actually legal! Thankfully it was, by the fact that there was no doubt *who* I was. However, it goes without saying that my birth and marriage certificates have never matched, but thankfully this did not cause a problem until I was in my forties and required a passport. That application turned out to be quite a fiasco!

During the first year or so of our marriage Mum and Gran still had quite a hefty input to our lives. I would be chastised if I went a couple of days without ringing them up, and they still expected me to do what they instructed, although it wasn't as bad as when I had been at home. They thought going on camping holidays was dreadful and seemed to consider we would be struck down by goodness knows what dreadful illnesses as a result of taking fresh air! I visited them after work once a week and tried to be a dutiful daughter, although conversations seemed rather stilted in those days. There were many questions I wished to ask, but I knew from bitter experience they would not be answered, and so I did not pursue the matter.

As time passes though, things tend to come to a head, and this situation certainly did. Ian and I were expecting our first baby in autumn 1971 and upon attending antenatal classes I was asked for family medical history. Obviously, I couldn't tell the doctor or midwives a single thing about my past apart from the childhood illnesses I remembered having myself. One midwife in particular was quite snooty about it, stating I should have 'known' about possible inherited diseases. How?

My biggest fear was telling Mum and Gran about the coming event. Ridiculous really, over a forthcoming happy event, and it truly told of the hold they had over me – even when I was married. I knew them well enough to know how they felt about 'men' in general and they would be quite judgemental instead of looking at it as a pleasure in having a first grandchild. I was right. I could have written a book about the weird and scary things Gran told me about *her* pregnancy with Mum: being 'bound up' and all sorts of mysterious or dreadful experiences to anticipate. It did occur to me that my mum (to my knowledge) had never even been pregnant, so how could *she* deliver such awful forebodings? Thankfully, I had the sense to book in for pre-natal classes, where I learnt all the things I needed to know. Mum and Gran did not approve of my 'being so involved' with other women in such a 'condition'. Still, having a baby in 1912 was very different from having one in 1972! These comments did frighten me somewhat, which made me think even more about my own origins and my acquisition. I really thought I would never to be able to find out.

Our first baby, Margaret Lesley, was born on the 7th of June 1972. I could not believe this beautiful healthy baby was mine. In those days new mothers stayed in hospital for several days following a birth, and it gave me plenty of time to sit and hold her, gaze into her beautiful face with absolute disbelief that she was the first 'blood' relative I had ever seen. She looked so much like me it was amazing, and I couldn't wait to take her home.

I guess – as was to be expected – Mum and Gran 'took over'. They arrived at the hospital on the day I was discharged with the baby, and had a taxi waiting. All I wanted was for Ian to come for us and to take our baby home together. I found out later that he had been given his 'orders' and rather than upset me he had gone to a cricket match to keep out of the way! Once we arrived home they stayed until he returned home, when at last we had little Margaret to ourselves. This sort of intrusion was quite common and regular, but both Ian and I had been only children, and had both been brought up to respect and obey our parents, although he was far more independent that I was. We were also both still very shy, neither of us possessing the grit or (I suppose) anger to stick up for ourselves, which really was ridiculous. Still, I guess Mum and Gran's reasoning was actually to help, but it was such a pity they were so dominant and controlling.

Naturally I received plenty of advice from them regarding

Our first daughter, Margaret Lesley, born 7th June, 1972.

the baby's upbringing, but I continued to attend the clinic regularly where I found helpful people. It wasn't all 'doom and gloom', but given half a chance my two matriarchs would have taken over completely. One strange thing Mum said to me when she first saw Margaret was 'You looked just like that when you were born.' That of course made me start wondering just how old I was when I had been adopted, or fostered? Had they known my birth mother, and how on earth could she have given me away? Something deep inside told me that she must have had no choice, for I would have killed to keep my baby if anyone had tried to take her away. I was still too young and immature really to know or realise that sort of thing had gone on for years – as many modern television programmes now show of course on *Long Lost Family* and *Who Do You Think You Are?*. The tragedy and heartache for so many young mothers – many of them completely innocent in an age where 'things' were not discussed – was dreadful.

Those first two years of Margaret's life, watching her grow and develop, became the happiest time of my life, and my happiness increased a hundredfold with the birth of our second little girl, Helen Ruth, when Margaret was three years old. Obviously with my childhood history I had never been around young children or babies, so their milestones and development were miraculous to me. Mum and Gran's comments and gloomy predictions returned during the months of waiting for Helen's arrival, but despite being ten days overdue she was born during a July heatwave and initially was a carbon copy of her older sister. This time Ian met us at the hospital as Mum and Gran stayed at home to look after Margaret. I wanted Ian to carry the new baby in so I could give Margaret a special hug when we arrived, but she ran straight down the stairs to see her new baby sister, bypassing me completely!

This new baby was a completely different kettle of fish. For one thing she slept like an angel, whereas Margaret had always been a bad sleeper. As Helen grew, it was obvious she was not going to let her older sister do anything she couldn't do! She was on her feet at six months, walking at ten months and attempting to climb the balustrade rails on the stairs, as well as chattering and trying to out-talk everyone. Very strong-willed, always having to have the 'last word' or 'action'. My mum's old school chum Auntie Marjorie always said Helen was 'born grown-up'. She never needed to be told how to act, how to be polite or behave in company. She was an old head in a young body.

These were not the only things very noticeable about our second daughter. Although Margaret had black hair when she was born, it was soon replaced by beautiful fair strawberry-blonde tresses. She was fair-skinned, had numerous freckles and lovely hazel-brown eyes which had a glimmer of gold in the centre. Helen, on the other hand, was much darker. She was born with the same black hair as Margaret but Helen's grew very rapidly, remained black and turned into long natural curly ringlets. Her skin was olive, her

Our second daughter Helen Ruth, born 21 July, 1975.

eyes almost black like her hair, and no one would have believed they were 'full' sisters. In fact, Helen looked nothing like Ian or I, whereas Margaret always resembled myself. There was no doubt I had the right baby, but many people asked if they had 'different fathers' as they grew up.

One incident occurred which haunted me for a long time. Mum and Dad (after Gran passed away) lived opposite a lovely family who had a son and daughter. Their mother was Italian and their father Portuguese. We were all invited to the Christening celebration of their little girl and that day found ourselves in a room full of Italian men. At that time Helen was two years old; she wore a red pleated dress and had huge red ribbons tying up her curly hair in bunches. Quite a number of the men admired both little girls, but when they saw Helen all we could hear was 'Poca Bella' meaning 'Little Beauty – 'Italiano'. I kept walking round the room saying both the little girls were mine, sisters, but they still kept pointing at Helen and exclaiming about her. At that point Mum got quite ruffled, and we all left without any explanation – once more the seeds of doubt were planted in my mind that Mum may have known or suspected far more about my past than she was willing to tell me.

Certainly I had no doubt now that somewhere in my past I must have had either Spanish or Italian origins, but of course I didn't know or have the courage of just how to pursue this. Life was far too busy looking after the children – I had them seven days a week, day and night, as Ian worked a permanent night-shift from the first year we were married, and every single day now because I was not working I was expected to go round to Mum's for lunch.

In the months before Helen was born we had discovered that Gran had glaucoma and had already lost the sight in one eye. Sadly the sight in her other eye could not be saved, so Mum and Gran decided they would move to be nearer to Ian and I. They therefore were only a five minute walk away by the time Helen was born, and the routine had become a daily occurrence. I had no problem in visiting and allowing Mum and Gran to enjoy the children of course, as sadly Gran never actually saw Helen. Still she really enjoyed having the baby on her knee and cuddling her. I wonder if she cuddled me as a baby – she probably did! Still, I don't remember any of that emotional bonding as I grew up.

Gran died when Helen was two and Margaret five, and now Mum required female company. Dad had retired so he was there all the time, but she never really enjoyed his sole company. She was happiest in the company of other women and even persuaded Ian's parents to take a week's cottage holiday with them. I could not understand why she found Dad's company lacking in some way, for he was such a wonderful person, but no – another woman was the best company for her. He wanted to take her on coach holidays all over the country but she refused. She didn't like being with groups of people – all the years with Gran had more than likely stuck her in this mental attitude and without her mother she was lost. Dad said to me at the time Gran died, 'Perhaps your Mum and I can do things now.' But no – it was too late. She was stuck in a rut and remained in it for the rest of her life.

Taking the little ones round to her house each day now became her hub. She never really talked to me, but I know she loved seeing the children grow, and once Margaret started school Mum and Dad would come with me to meet her in an afternoon, and then we would go back to their house for a while. This was fine until it became a situation whereby every day I would receive a telephone call from Mum to say 'dinner was ready'. I didn't have the heart to refuse as Dad obviously did all the cooking and I didn't want to hurt his feelings, but it soon became a something of a trap for me. By the time Helen started school at the age of four I was summonsed every day for lunch, sat with Mum until it was time to meet the girls from school – and so it went on for over a year. I was 'climbing the walls' as I wanted the freedom to find some sort of work or occupation now the children were growing up a bit, but how could I escape?

My salvation partly came as a result of finding legal work to do at home. With still having many penfriends and a good typewriter I had kept up my speed and accuracy, so I advertised amongst local solicitors for some sort of work which would fit in with Ian's shifts and the school runs. Thankfully I received good work engrossing long legal leases of thirty-pages or more which in those days without photocopiers, computers and word processors were a laborious job which took up too much time in office hours. This freelance work meant that my brain could be concentrated on something positive, and of course the little bit of extra money came in very useful. It meant I could genuinely go round to my parents' house a bit later and then go directly home after collecting the girls in order to finish off work. Mum was not happy about this, but Dad certainly was and he encouraged me to 'keep my hand in', as he put it.

The years were passing quickly – we had wonderful holidays and over the years had advanced from the scout tent to various frame tents, then trailer-tents and finally caravans. We never went abroad in those days, but travelled the length and breadth of the country from Land's End to John O'Groats, sharing all the childhood years of our lovely daughters. I admit I found it very hard work sometimes – especially when the children were very young, or with the British weather and perpetual rain, but it was true precious family time. During the rest of the year, Sunday was the only day we had together as a family with Ian working permanent night-shifts.

As I watched the children grow I became more and more focused on wanting to know just where I came from. Not only that – who were their birth grandparents? Where did they come from? Who did Helen look like? Even more – who did I look like? Helen's personality was definitely very similar to mine, but her flashing black eyes, long black hair and ability to dance were outstanding. Margaret shared many similarities to myself and her dad and was very shy as a young child, but Helen more than made up for that! I never could believe they were both mine – how lucky I was.

Needless to say, I never exerted the sort of claustrophobic upbringing on them such as I had received. I felt it was essential for them to be just who they were, to be reasonably streetwise and *talk* to them both about everything and anything. Ian was very involved with them too and they loved their Dad very much.

The niggle of just 'who' I was had grown enormously since the birth of my girls. However, Mum and Dad were still there, and I couldn't do anything at all. I still feel that Dad would have been quite interested to assist me in looking into my origins and even give me advice of how to go about it, but Mum's inflexibility made this impossible. She was also getting much older and I had no wish to upset or distress her in any way. Also, I did wonder if involving Dad in attempting to find out about my 'natural' family might hurt him too? I would never have done that. So, anything I did had to be completely secret.

And so my conscience of deceitfulness was about to take over, and was something which never went away from that moment when I found courage to make the first step towards discovery.

I made that first step when the girls were two and five years old. We had been camping just outside London and I mentioned to Ian that I would like to visit St. Catherine's House, where birth records were kept in those days. The girls were too young to realise the importance of what I was doing or to relay this incident to my mum, so it felt reasonably safe. I thought if I could obtain a full copy of my birth certificate it might throw some light on my parentage or where I came from, but when I filled the form in at the register office the realisation of what I was doing really overwhelmed me. It was simply so easy! After being directed to the huge register book in question, there was my birth name listed against 16 February 1948 with a reference number. I felt quite shaky handing the fee over, but was told the full certificate would be posted out to me in around three days' time.

This was a bit worrying, as Mum and Dad always went round to our house whilst we were away to pick any post up and check everything was in order, and I was concerned that any envelope from St. Catherine's House might have that address stamped on the outside. I knew from sad past experience that if any correspondence for me was discovered which Mum thought was her business she would not hesitate in opening it! In my teenage years Mum and Gran had on several occasions withheld letters to me from penfriends and written to these people themselves telling them not to correspond with me anymore. Nothing was private, and I only discovered what was going on when one of those penfriends had telephoned me at work to see what was wrong! Thankfully my concern this time was unfounded, as the envelope did not bear any relevant information as to its contents.

However, the contents of the envelope were something else. I stood there with my full birth certificate in my hand, and for the first time at the age of twenty-nine discovered something about myself. But it would still take a lifetime for everything to unfold.

CHAPTER 6

Information At Last

My hands were shaking as I slit open the envelope containing my full birth certificate. Yes, I did feel guilty. Very guilty. It was almost as if I had no right to read this birth certificate – my conscience had been so thoroughly trained throughout my childhood that although Gran was now in care it still felt as if Mum would be able to see right through me, tell Gran and know what I had done – as if I was transparent.

The emotions which teemed through my mind as I tried to absorb the information before me were immense. I don't know what I had expected, but I couldn't take it in properly. There in front of me were *three* addresses and the name of my birth mother (father unknown). My birth mother was called Vera May.

Three addresses. What did they mean? Obviously one of them – 89 North Road, Wolverhampton – must have been where my birth mother was living. 376 Wolverhampton Road, Heath Town – what was that? According to the certificate that is where I was born, so perhaps Vera was staying with friends or family there? The Flat, Saighton Hall was my birth mother's home address apparently, so what was 89 North Road? This was all very confusing. And where was Saighton Hall? It sounded like something from *Upstairs Downstairs*. With my active imagination I had too much rushing through it – possibilities, nonsense, where, what, who?

All our lives we make suppositions and guesses about

things. I couldn't have been more wrong about my initial assumptions, but it was going to take a long time before I knew everything!

Before the days of internet it was really difficult to discover information – which is available at the touch of a button nowadays. I attempted to find Saighton Hall, but nothing was mentioned anywhere, it seemed. Ian knew that the village of Saighton was somewhere near Chester – his post office training meant he knew virtually every city, town, village, hamlet or homestead in the country, so at least that was something. So, Chester seemed to be involved in my background, which was incredible as I had been there a few times; when I began driving it was a place Mum and Gran loved to go. The memory came back to me immediately of Saighton Camp, which Dad had wished to visit, and the strange behaviour of Mum and Gran that day. Had they known something? I had always felt an affinity and connection when we visited such a beautiful place, and it seemed now as if that could be where I came from! Quite strange!

Chester is a place of wonder. I have always adored 'olde worlde' places, so the Roman, Saxon, Tudor, Georgian and Victorian buildings, the fabulous River Dee and the preserved city walls had woven their magic around me even as a teenager on a school trip (the only one I was ever allowed to make!).

During the following twelve years that new certificate was brought out and examined many times, with all sorts of ideas and fancies teeming through my head. Of course 'Saighton' was not a widely known or obvious place, so that link with Dad visiting the old army camp there and 'Saighton Hall' on the certificate instilled in me all sorts of thoughts – improbable and otherwise. Guesswork is never much use, and it is so easy to build up a story in one's mind a million miles from the truth. I needed some concrete information and evidence. Although I held in my hand such a wealth of information I did not have the courage to do anything about

The Family in 1986.

it, being acutely aware that Mum and Dad must not discover it was in my possession.

The girls kept me very busy as they grew up; we took many camping holidays, had happy and sad times as every family does, and during these years we moved to a larger house a mile up the road from Mum and Dad. Mum never forgave us for this – when Gran passed away she was not quite as assertive towards me as previously, but she could still twist the mental screws very nicely. She had always sent Christmas and birthday cards to the girls signed 'Love from Grandma and Grandad round the corner'. Upon on our move the cards simply said 'With love from Grandma and Grandad NOT round the corner'! Oh dear! Considering I could be with them in under five minutes by car it was not the end of the world, but that was how Mum thought. She never forgave us for that move. I could not bear to consider what effect it would have on her (Dad would probably have been reasonable and accepting) if she discovered my deceitfulness. I had not reached the point where I felt it was my 'right' to know about my past – that didn't happen until another thirty or forty years passed by. It may sound ridiculous, but everything that had gone before really coloured my conscience and ability to 'get on' with things.

However, there was one incident. Every year we visited Ian's aunt, who lived in Fareham, Hampshire. In those days when our children were young it was a very long drive – it could take about seven hours. When Margaret and Helen were about eight and five years old, I asked Ian if we could take in a detour through Saighton on the journey down south, or even Wolverhampton, where I had been born. He happily took out his maps (he could spend hours studying them – it was one of his most popular hobbies), and thought we could do so quite easily.

I was still very curious about both places mentioned on my certificate. Although it made the journey longer, we did make small detours and drove through both areas on that journey. We found Saighton just outside the city of Chester, and found a place to park on a triangle of grass at the end of the village to have our picnic. Saighton was a pretty, quiet little village consisting of one long road. It felt very peculiar to know I was somewhere my birth mother had actually lived, but we had no idea where Saighton Hall was. Our picnic was taken outside a very large building entitled 'Abbey Gate College', but there were no signs or directions to 'Saighton Hall'. The village itself didn't seem to be very big, and as Ian was anxious to continue our journey we didn't have time to make enquiries or look around. I just scribbled a few notes, wondering how long my birth mother had lived there – and indeed was she *still* there? Had I ever been there?

Recommencing our journey, Wolverhampton was another story altogether. Ian found 'North Road' on his map, and this was at a time before the infamous ring road was built. We drove up North Road but it was obvious a lot of buildings had been demolished and the only ones still intact were built of stone and were very dingy. We turned right by the side of an old school but that is the only thing I remember about that particular visit, and it did not enlighten me at all about 89 North Road. I could only assume it had been demolished.

These visits were the only snippets of information I had, and it was not until 1988 I made any further enquiries.

Life had been so busy during the intervening years and I felt reasonably satisfied that I had actually visited Saighton. The girls grew up, my working at home evolved into part-time work and then full-time work in offices once more and life was busy, active and, at times, quite hectic.

The first years in our new house were good, but then a lot of problems started to raise their heads, throwing my life into turmoil. These revolved mainly around our four parents – Ian's were now in their late eighties, and my parents were in their early eighties. My mother and father-in-law were lovely people and we visited them regularly every week during the years the girls were growing up, and they came to us at Christmas and special times. They were quite aware of the difficulties with Mum and Gran and had frequently kept their opinions to themselves in order to keep the peace.

Over a two-year period it became more and more difficult to cope with our parents' various difficulties, work full time and oversee two teenage daughters. Ian and I were both 'only' children, and of course as he worked nights he was not really available for long during the weekdays. Ian's parents were the biggest worry initially, and their health issues resulted in them moving to a nursing home very close to my parents, but sadly during that period we lost both of them.

The concerns with my parents covered the following three to four years, so it was almost like being in a maelstrom of a nightmare at times. Obviously this happens to many people – being in the middle of difficult teenagers on the one hand and ailing parents on the other. One can only do what is necessary and to the best of their abilities, but I remember this period of time with complete dismay and serious depression.

Things went from bad to worse when we discovered that Margaret was pregnant at the age of sixteen and a half. This was another cause of extreme anxiety, and there were times when it seemed nothing would ever be 'normal' again.

And so New Year 1989 arrived, and Margaret's baby was due that September. Little did I know 'Pandora's Box' was about to be opened! My mind was spinning even more at the prospect of a grandchild being born, and all the old thoughts and questions reared themselves again. Here was a baby who was going to come into the world the same way I did – except that it would have a devoted birth mother, a family home, grandparents and great grandparents, as both sets of parents were still alive then. Margaret had been given the options of either keeping the baby with our support or letting it go for adoption, but I knew she would never have taken that road. If the baby arrived safely we would add another member to our family. It was frightening having to advise Mum of Margaret's situation but she sniffed and made it quite clear how disgusting it was. I think she felt I had failed my daughter, which did nothing for my ego!

One day, on a complete impulse, I took out my birth certificate once more, and studied it carefully. I guess it was a sort of 'release' from what was going on around me – to try and concentrate on something else, but I made a decision to attempt to discover anything I could about *my* birth mother. It seemed her true address was The Flat, Saighton Hall where she was employed as doing general domestic duties at the time of my birth. My mind wandered back to our brief visit at the time of our picnic when the largest property we had seen in Saighton was Abbey Gate College. But if that was the case, why was she living at 89 North Road when I was born? And what was 376 Wolverhampton Road?

This was not a decision taken lightly at all. If I did continue and discovered anything it would have to be a total secret from Mum and Dad, which felt very deceitful. Almost twelve years had passed since I acquired my full birth certificate, and the girls were now almost fourteen and seventeen. I considered they were old enough to know what I wished to do. They were not only very interested but encouraged me to do so. I felt they were trustworthy enough not to blurt out any of it to their grandparents, and they assured me they would keep it private between us.

Ian's attitude was that it didn't really matter – but as I pointed out to him he knew his own family tree going back to 1555 at the time of the Marian Persecutions, and knew he had been born in the front room of his family home. When I asked him how he would feel if he knew nothing whatsoever about his birth family or, indeed, didn't know who he really was, he did come to understand.

My closest friend from the age of five, Lynne, knew all about the situation and she also knew about my childhood and the rod of iron Mum and Gran had ruled with. She was very encouraging about my idea to try and discover something of my past.

And so, after one particularly difficult day, I simply sat down at my typewriter and addressed a letter to the bursar of Abbey Gate College in Saighton. I explained how I thought this building had perhaps been the old Saighton Hall where Vera had been in domestic service, and asked if anyone there had memories of Vera May Ashton (my birth mother) from the 1940s. I stated I was doing family genealogy (which was true) but that I had hit a brick wall. I enclosed a stamped addressed envelope, and then found myself in a quandary as I simply could not bring myself to post the letter, being too scared of what I was about to do. Neither could I rip it up. This was monumental! I carried that letter around with me for about five weeks, before suddenly stopping the car one day, handing it to Helen and asking her to put it into a letterbox! My conscience had got the better of me after one day being pushed to the limits of my endurance with Mum, and somehow it just felt it didn't matter anymore. Just do it!

I never thought for a moment this action would lead to anything positive. In those days I had an extremely negative outlook, which probably was left over from my formative years, but amazingly a few weeks later my stamped addressed envelope fell through the letterbox. I recognised it immediately. I picked it up and, sitting on the bottom stair with trembling hands, slit it open. The thin piece of paper inside was from a gentleman who lived in Saighton who remembered Vera well, and not only gave me her married name but her actual address in Crewe, of all places! This was unbelievable. She was now called Mrs Roberts, and he told me Saighton Hall had been the name of the farm where my birth family had lived in a flat during the war years.

When my letter had arrived at Abbey Gate College no one knew anything, so it seems the bursar had kindly taken it down to the post office in Saighton Village where it had been posted on the notice board. This is how the gentleman who remembered Vera had been able to contact me.

Gosh, what a situation! So, my birth mother was still alive, and living only around 35 miles away! This situation now put me in a real quandary as to whether to simply accept the facts or take the matter further. Of course, the girls wanted me to go ahead to see if I could contact her, but Ian was rather more careful. He pointed out many things which were sensible, and of course I realised myself that she may not want to know me in the first instance, or that as she was obviously married her family may not know anything about me being the 'skeleton in the cupboard'. I was not capable of marching up to a stranger's front door without warning and announcing I was her daughter! That would be most inconsiderate and wrong.

Lynne, however, had no qualms about the matter. 'You have to try and find out now,' she said. 'You can't leave it at this.' I mulled over it day after day, knowing that if Mum found out she would be so distressed and in total denial. Dad may have actually been interested and helpful, but it was impossible to share any discoveries with them in the circumstances. After all, Mum and Dad were my parents – giving birth to a child does not automatically make good parents, and my foster parents had given me a good home and upbringing, regardless of how difficult I found it at times. I had been given good clothes, lots of toys, and a wonderful father, and I believe a certain lack of knowledge about bringing up a child had been the cause of some problems I had encountered. I had been very lucky indeed but they were definitely over-protective for some unknown reason. There was no wish in my mind to 'replace' the Mum and Dad I had always known, but simply to find out where I came from and literally who I was. Mum and Gran would never have understood that as they would have considered – as in many things – that it was nothing to do with me, but thankfully in our modern day and age it is understood that people not only wish to know these things, but that they have the right to do so! There was nothing so reassuring for me though at that time, unfortunately.

Therefore, after a time of great deliberation, disturbed sleep and soul searching I haltingly contacted social services and asked for an appointment to discuss the matter. I spoke to a lovely lady called Ms S., who interviewed me and took some details. A few days later she made some enquiries which confirmed that Vera Roberts was, indeed, the same Vera Ashton from Saighton, and told me that if I decided to take the matter further she herself would write a letter to Vera in terms only she would understand. Should anyone else read it they would not know who I was or anything about me. Apparently this was what social services did regularly at that time on behalf of anonymous children who wished to contact their birth parents. Had I been legally adopted this situation would have been far more difficult and laborious, but with having my original birth certificate and never having been legally adopted it was much easier.

So, should I or shouldn't I go ahead? Again Lynne encouraged me, and so did Ian, who by this time was quite curious himself. I knew, however, that if I took the next step and if Vera wished to meet up with me, there could be no going back and she would have to accept my anonymity during my parents' lifetimes. My conscience was pricking very painfully. Margaret and Helen, who realised the seriousness of the matter, were both very anxious to know what was, in any event, their ancestry as well as mine – and, as Margaret said, her baby's history as well!

At a second interview with Ms S. I revealed how I felt, and explained about my misgivings. She smiled and said that was natural, but here was the opportunity to discover more and her advice was to go ahead. She reassured me it would all be done very discreetly and that no addresses or information about me would be given to Vera should she wish to meet me. That would be for me to decide at a later time.

Ms S. duly sent the letter to Vera, and amazingly received a telephone call the very next day asking when Vera could meet me, and to 'make it as soon as possible please'. This was mind-blowing. When I haltingly agreed, Ms S. made a reservation to take me to the council offices in Crewe, where special rooms were designated for these meetings.

For the first time in my life I threw a 'sicky' from work, the meeting being arranged for a Friday, and Ms S. drove me to Crewe where, on the 2nd of March 1989, for the first time at the age of forty-one, I met my birth mother.

CHAPTER 7

My Birth Mother

On the 7th of July 1989 whilst waiting for Ms S. on the morning I was due to meet Vera, my birth mother, I could not have described to anyone just how this felt. How surreal it was – this couldn't be happening to me, could it? However, 9 a.m. arrived after a very restless night, and Ms S. collected me and we set off for Crewe. The meeting between Vera and I was scheduled for 11 a.m.

When we arrived, after a long chat en route in which Ms S. had told me of various successes and failures in these situations, she instructed me to stay in the car briefly whilst she checked that Vera had arrived and was in the appropriate room waiting for us. After a few minutes Ms S. came running back to the car after 'booking us in', and excitedly told me she knew Vera was there – she had seen a lady standing at the reception and there was 'No doubt who she was, we looked so alike!' Gosh!

Ms S. advised me that she would stay with Vera and myself for around half an hour to ensure things were 'all right' between us, and if they were she would then leave us in privacy for an hour or so. If things were not 'working out', she would tactfully draw me out of the room without upsetting Vera.

So, with a pounding heart and shaky legs I accompanied Ms S. up the stairs at the council offices. As it had been Vera's sixtieth birthday the previous day I arrived with a large bouquet of flowers. Obviously, Vera had only been nineteen when I was born.

My birth mother Vera.

As I entered the room, Vera was sitting by the window. She turned her head, looked at me, and just said 'It's you. Yes it is, it's you.' I was completely overwhelmed by this stranger – the woman who had actually given birth to me. I was not identical to her but the likeness was amazing, so obviously no mistake had been made; this *was* my birth mother. As I took a seat opposite to her I simply didn't know what to say. I am not often lost for words, but this was completely unreal, and in a way a little disturbing.

Ms S. had ordered refreshments, and we made a tentative attempt at conversation. I had so many questions I wanted to ask, but it seemed rude to just 'dive in' and begin cross-examining a complete stranger, so we exchanged normal pleasantries and I told Vera something about my family – she was delighted to receive the news she was a grandmother and, indeed, about to become a great-grandmother too. She was very reticent to say much to me, so I had to tread carefully and attempt to draw some information out of her. I realised this must be difficult for Vera, but I was desperate to know 'something'.

Over a very welcome pot of tea and biscuits, which were brought in to us, things grew a little easier. Ms S. realised we were getting along quite reasonably, so she excused herself and left us alone, saying she would return in half an hour. I was absolutely fascinated at the similarities between myself and my birth mother: how we sat, several little mannerisms and even in the way we dressed quite similarly. She was quite delicately built and not as tall as myself – probably around 5 ft 4' or so – but we had the same dark eyes and hair. We were definitely not 100% identical but there was something in the structure of our faces which revealed our relationship without a doubt. Vera had scars on the side of her face and neck so I began to suspect her life had been very difficult.

Obviously the biggest question on my mind was about my 'real' father, and it took a bit of courage to raise the subject as there was no doubt I had been illegitimate. In the 1940s this was a real stigma and disgrace of course. Trying to be as tactful as possible, I proffered the tentative question, making it clear I would understand if she did not wish to tell me anything. However her eyes immediately lit up and she then threw a really unexpected spanner into the works –she told me he was known as 'Charlie' and had been an Italian prisoner of war who worked in the potato fields alongside her on the farm in Saighton at the end of World War II. She went on to say that she simply knew him as 'Charlie', and that as he could not speak English she knew nothing more about him. They had met in the Rake and Pikel, a public house a few hundred yards from Saighton Army Camp, it seemed.

When I reflected on this information in the following weeks it did seem a bit strange, but obviously I was more than satisfied with what she had told me and at that time had no reason to doubt what I was told. With regard to the army camp I got goosebumps, as I knew my dad had trained there at the beginning of the war. Now it appeared my birth father had been in the same camp at the end of the war! Amazing.

This information took my breath away – I was half Italian – and here was the solution as to why my daughters looked so completely different! Margaret with her fair strawberry-blonde hair and fair skin, and Helen with black eyes, black hair and olive skin! My eldest daughter obviously took after me and my youngest daughter had inherited around 99% of her grandfather's Italian heritage! Not only the looks, but her natural ability to dance – the Italian genes must have passed down through me.

Both of my girls and myself have always had the Italian love of architecture, art, classical music and beautiful scenery, which I suspect could also have come from that direction. It was a monumental discovery for me on that day. This was the answer as to why Mum and Gran were never, ever, going to succeed in 'moulding' me into being the same as them. They never had, and never would, have succeeded in understanding me as a person. I might not have looked Italian outwardly, but had always been over-sensitive and volatile; not in the sense of having a temper, but in the way I feel emotions so deeply and love to express things by waving my hands around, writing at length, composing poems and sometimes going 'well over the top' in appreciation of words, beauty and life itself as well as being extremely analytical. That is debatable of course, but a definite possibility. Vera told me Charlie was a very 'gentle' young man, tall and good looking. I got the distinct impression she had loved him a great deal.

The main information Vera gave to me was that she had been the second eldest of six children. Three girls followed by three boys, and that her older sister, Joan, had died at the age of forty-seven. She also told me she had been badly burnt all down her right side at the age of fourteen. The story was that upon leaving school her father had put her into service locally, and one day whilst setting a fire the corner of her apron had caught alight and she had spent several months thereafter in hospital having skin grafts. I did not realise until much later at other meetings just how bad this had been. Sadly the accident and its results left her badly epileptic, which I gathered had greatly affected her life. My heart went out to her, as I started to see what a sad life she had experienced from such a young age. I wondered if her condition was the reason she had not been able to keep me, but it was far too soon to approach that particular subject.

I did manage to figure out that Vera was now married to a Mr Roberts, but it was difficult to draw any more out as I felt I was intruding on her private life in asking personal questions. Vera had not enquired much about my parents, but I did tell her briefly that I had enjoyed a secure childhood and she expressed thanks to them for taking me in. I also explained it was impossible to invite her into my family at this point because I had not been able to share her discovery with them. Vera told me she completely understood and was just happy we had made contact.

Trying to pluck up courage, as the time was passing quickly, I managed to ask her if I had any siblings. She replied that during her first marriage when she lived in Northern Ireland, she had a son and daughter, but then with tears in her eyes told me that they had died – along with their father – in a house fire as babies. I was completely stunned, and could only press her hand in sympathy and tried to show understanding for this tragedy. Obviously I did not push for more information, as I reckoned the only way she could cope with such a situation was to close a door on the past. She did, however, tell me they had been called Robert and Carolyn.

I did not wish to go into too much 'digging for information' at this first meeting, and of course it was not a situation where one could have a list of questions to ask.

After the above unsuspected information and the emotional aftermath of the meeting I certainly had more than enough to take in for the moment. Ms S. returned after the aforesaid half an hour and although I did not divulge any information to Vera about my home, I did tell her I lived in the Manchester area and we exchanged telephone numbers. Vera asked me quite profoundly to promise I would now keep in touch and eventually take my family to meet her.

To say I sat in silence on the ride home in Ms S.'s car was the understatement of the year! She enquired as to what I had been told, as she was greatly interested, but she did warn me that people did not always tell the truth when meeting long-lost children. I did not take that on board, but over the next few years her words of premonition certainly came true.

Ian and the girls were avidly interested in my meeting of course, and I told them all I could remember. Like me, they were astonished at the revelation of one half of our family being Italian, but from that moment on Helen 'gave in' to her Italian side. She had always loved to dress in bright colours, dance to her heart's content, wear ra-ra skirts and put a flower in her long dark hair. It was so easy for her! It is certainly true that genetically people cannot always deny their heritage! Now she was determined to enjoy it properly!

Following our first meeting, Vera and I had several telephone conversations over quite a long time, and as is often the case sometimes it is easier to talk that way rather than face to face. I began to build up more of a picture regarding my early life as Vera told me she had been 'sent away' for my birth so that explained the reason I was born in Wolverhampton in the West Midlands whilst my birth family lived just outside Chester.

At the time I met Vera there were no television programmes about *Long Lost Family* or *Who Do You Think You Are*, as otherwise I would probably have realised she had been sent to a mother and baby home, being unmarried and pregnant, but after many more years passed I would learn all about this side of things. She was adamant that 'Charlie' had known about her expecting a baby, but followed this up with the news that the 'entire Italian contingent' were returned to Italy without notice in the August of 1947 when she was around three or four months pregnant with me. Obviously I checked this out, and the information was true that the last Italians left England at that time – apart from many, I believe, who stayed and made their future lives in the UK.

It has taken me virtually a lifetime to work out where huge gaps in the 'life jigsaw' could be filled in, which at this particular time were missing. Vera did tell me, however, over the next few weeks and months that I had three 'real' uncles and an aunt who were still alive, and obviously a lot of first cousins. This was amazing, having been brought up in a completely 'contained' family of just four people including myself, to now upon reaching my forties have an unknown number of blood relatives scattered around. I was not ready to be introduced to any of this family yet though, and had impressed upon Vera that I was unable not only to invite her to my home but indeed tell anyone we had met. Because of the likenesses between us I could not have passed her off as a 'friend', as it was only too obvious we were closely related. She seemed to completely understand this and was simply so happy to have met the eldest daughter she had lost.

Vera was so anxious for us to pay her a visit, we actually did go to Crewe on the 5th August – just a month after we had met and just a month before her great-grandchild was born. This felt very strange indeed, but she insisted and although my guilt was very strong at still being so deceitful, the girls wanted so much to meet their birth grandmother so we made the arrangement to visit Vera at her home in Crewe.

At the time of meeting Vera she was married to a Mr Ken Roberts, who seemed very nice, but she had told us he had a bad temper at times. However we found him to have quite a pleasant personality and he made us very welcome. He obviously was considerably older than Vera and we felt he had a few 'learning' difficulties. Vera's younger sister, Betty, came to meet us and she was so lovely – Margaret and Auntie Betty had the same beautiful strawberry-blonde hair! The two sisters had put on a huge buffet for us and a 'welcome' cake. In future years Auntie Betty would become a big part of my family, but that was as yet on the horizon and many years and situations would occur in the meantime.

The meeting went well and the girls were enthralled to meet a birth relative. One thing sticks in my mind about that visit to her lovely home in Crewe, as I read a verse in a frame above the table. This was about 'People who adopt a child' – that is all I can remember, but is something which, many years later, really came back to haunt me.

And so something I had never thought possible had happened: I had not only found, but also met, my birth mother. So much was spinning around in my head with such a lot of information I still wanted to know, but already I had started to learn that Vera was capable of changing her little stories if she felt it appropriate, and Auntie Betty actually warned me about this. So, it was also a matter of taking things in and trying to establish which of them were true, and I decided to stay with the facts which were obviously correct and go on from there.

In some ways I wish I had taken things further at that time. However, it was not possible because I loved my Mum and Dad and did not wish to hurt either of them, and I was also frightened of the consequences regarding Mum should she discover what I had done. Still, there were no regrets and at the appropriate future time a real 'Pandora's Box' would open for me.

One thing which was completely outstanding upon our first visit to Vera's home was when Helen walked through the door for the first time and Vera saw her. In a completely spontaneous reaction, Vera looked up, saw Helen, and went as white as a sheet. 'Oh, Charlie,' she breathed, completely devoid of words.

CHAPTER 8

Light and Darkness

———

And so – what did I know for sure? My birth mother, Vera, had met my father, Charlie, who was an Italian prisoner of war on the farm where her family were living and working at the time in 1947. Vera and her parents, older sister Joan, younger sister Betty and three younger brothers Albert, Don and Eric, lived at Saighton Grange Farm in a tied flat as they worked on the land. This was the post-war era, and I was told Vera met Charlie when he was working in the potato fields, which many POWs did until they were repatriated back to their own countries.

Vera and Charlie first met in the Rake and Pikel which is a very pretty public house at Huntington, a small village adjacent to Saighton, and which is a couple of hundred yards down the road from the old Saighton Army Camp. She told me they would walk down the country lanes approximately two miles back to the farm together and she described him as 'tall, handsome, lovely natured and slim'. I never did understand why she told me she knew nothing about where he came from in Italy or what his surname was. Maybe she had information she simply did not wish to pass on to me, or had forgotten! She also denied he could speak English, which is hard to believe as she said she knew him for two years, and as she said he visited her home frequently and her parents liked him; surely she would have known far more than she revealed?

I am able to believe what Vera said about not really being aware she was expecting a baby, as even in my own teenage years girls were kept very ignorant of the facts of life, which were never even mentioned. In the 1940s and even through to the 1960s it was essential to keep an unmarried girl's 'condition' secret from the neighbourhood.

And so we arrived at September 1989, just two months after meeting Vera for the first time. On the 7th of September we welcomed Margaret's new little son, Jamie, into the family. There had been some difficult times but he had arrived in the world just as I did – to an unmarried mother – except for one important thing: our grandson came into a loving family and we could never have ever imagined giving him up. He was absolutely beautiful, staring around the delivery room immediately with huge blue eyes within minutes of being born. It was like looking at an 'old head on young shoulders'. He rapidly became part of our family, adored by everyone including his young Auntie Helen, and we loved watching him grow and develop so quickly with all the attention and encouragement he received. He was laughing and chuckling by four weeks old, so despite her youth Margaret turned out to be a good mother who idolised her baby, and he was in a fair way to be spoilt – especially with the hitherto 'unknown' side of the family down in Crewe.

So for the time being life was full and happy. I had started a new job on a permanent four-hour a day basis with a boss I got along with really well, and who actually became a good friend during the next twenty-six years I worked for him. Ian was happy in his routine of night-shifts and weekends with the family, and my parents seemed to be coping well. As mentioned before, Ian's parents had by now moved from Droylsden to a care home just on the corner of Sycamore Avenue where my parents lived, so it was very easy for us to visit them all and they loved to see baby Jamie.

Vera and I held regular conversations and when Jamie was around six weeks old we managed to drive to Crewe and introduce her to her great-grandson. On our first visit with

With our first grandson Jamie.

Jamie, Auntie Betty had ordered a beautiful celebration cake for the occasion saying 'Welcome Jamie'. That was so lovely. Yes, life was bobbing along nicely, but as is always the case it seems the 'old wooden spoon' was stirring beneath the calm exterior and perhaps it was a good job at that time we did not realise what was about to befall us.

On Saturday the 7th of January 1990, the day baby Jamie was four months old, I had taken him into Ashton-under-Lyne with me to do some shopping, and as usual he was as good as gold, radiating gummy smiles as I spoke to him and tucked the covers around him. A cold January followed the happy Christmas we had spent at home, and having a young baby so intrigued at all the decorations and twinkling lights during the festive season had been even more enjoyable. When we arrived home that afternoon, Jamie seemed very sleepy and did not want his feed, and an hour or so later Margaret came running to me saying he had a very high temperature. Although we attempted to bring his temperature down, an hour or so later it was no better and so the emergency doctor was called. He arrived around 9 p.m., pronounced it was flu and handed

Margaret a prescription for penicillin. He also gave him a dose of penicillin by injection at the time.

The following day was Sunday, and as I have always been a believer that once started on a course of penicillin, it should be continued without a break thereafter, it would be lunchtime before we could get the remainder of the prescription – around fifteen hours later. We knew the local pharmacies would be closed, so Ian suggested we take a ride down into the centre of Manchester where there was an all-night pharmacy and that decision from Ian probably saved his grandson's life. It meant that we could give the baby further doses of antibiotics at 2 a.m. and 8 a.m. overnight. Lunchtime the following day (being a Sunday) would have been too late!

Margaret and I decided to sleep downstairs that night so we could take turns at keeping an eye on Jamie, whom we tucked up on the settee, and we shared an inflatable mattress on the lounge floor. The baby was quite restless, but at 2 a.m. after his second dose of penicillin he seemed to settle and go to sleep. When morning light was just peeping through the curtains Margaret was asleep so I checked Jamie, hoping that as night had subsided he would start to feel better, as so often happens. He was still in a deep sleep so I gently tried to rouse him and decided to change his Babygro to make him feel more comfortable. However he still felt very hot, and as I removed his Babygro I could see a dark red rash on his little body and limbs. I had never seen a rash like this, and my first thought was that it could be an allergy to the penicillin. Margaret had awoken by now and she walked up and down with him in her arms, trying to pacify and get him to take some boiled water or juice. We were not at all happy, so I telephoned the emergency doctor again and the telephonist said our own doctor was on emergency duty that morning and would call us back when he arrived.

Within half an hour of my changing Jamie his eyes rolled back into his head and he started to emit a high-pitched wailing noise, which was terrifying. At that moment our doctor phoned, and when I told him what was happening he ordered us to get down to the surgery immediately where he was doing some paperwork, and he would meet the car outside. Ian took Margaret and Jamie in the car, and when our doctor took one look at Jamie he ordered Ian to 'get the hell up to the hospital and don't stop for red lights.' Thankfully Ian did so, and Jamie was immediately rushed into the A & E department where the wonderful staff immediately ran tests and pumped him full of every conceivable antibiotic. Ian brought Margaret home about half an hour later to pack an overnight bag and to advise the rest of us that meningitis was suspected. I remember little after that as I sank to the floor in a sort of 'whiteout', and of course everyone was in deep shock. Margaret had been told he had a fifty-fifty chance of survival, but that was erring on the side of optimism! However, the gods were definitely with us as a cot in intensive care at Pendlebury Children's Hospital was found and with the assistance of two nurses and a doctor in the ambulance, who ministered whatever they possibly could to enhance his chances, mother and baby were transferred. With meningococcal meningitis and septicaemia every minute is crucial for survival as the bacteria multiply so quickly once the rash is present, and all we could hope was that the filthy disease had been caught quickly enough.

Everyone who had been in contact with Jamie for the previous week to ten days had to take a course of special strong antibiotics. Ian called the doctor to me as I was in shock, but when he gave me Valium and told me to stay and rest on the settee for three or four days I put the tablets down the toilet and drove over to Pendlebury Hospital to be with Margaret. I admit I was in a real haze and probably shouldn't have driven, but we both stayed there in the family rooms which were available for the four or five days the little soul fought for his life on a life support machine. The crucial time was when

Jamie was taken off the machine to see if he could by then support his own breathing. Thankfully he did, and all we could do was hope and pray he would recover, having come this far.

Much of the time spent going to and fro to the hospital, informing people of any progress, doing essential day-to-day jobs, visiting Jamie and sitting with him, talking and singing his familiar nursery rhymes in an attempt to stimulate his brain, was carried out in something of a fog for all of us. Time ceased to have any meaning and so did daily living, and it was dreadful to see our seventeen-year-old daughter going through such trauma. The staff at Pendlebury were absolutely wonderful, supportive and caring. Anyone who visited (no more than two at a time) had to scrub up before entering the intensive care ward and put on white coats and masks. On leaving the room these had to be taken off and hands scrubbed again.

The only person not allowed to visit Jamie was fourteen-year-old Helen, who also went through terrible trauma as it was hard for her playing the waiting game unable to see her little nephew. She was in her forties before she confided to me that she had always thought the doctors had discovered she was the 'carrier', and sadly I had not known this as she had not said anything to me at the time. I was mortified at this discovery, as the only reason she was not allowed to go into the unit was because no one under sixteen years of age was allowed, as teenagers are amongst one of the highest risks for meningitis and she could not have been allowed such exposure. It was upsetting to realise she had carried that thought for so long.

When it became obvious Jamie was holding his own a few days later, kind doctors arranged to transfer him to our local hospital, which was only three miles away. This made visiting much easier, as Pendlebury was sixteen miles away on the other side of Manchester. Although ambulance men had been on strike when we were told about the move, they kindly took it upon themselves to make this journey for us, which was greatly appreciated.

Margaret stayed with Jamie all day, every day, and after I finished my part-time work at 1 p.m. in those days I would go to sit with her for the afternoon. It was impossible to concentrate properly on anything during those days, as Jamie was as weak as a newborn baby now and slept most of the time, still linked up to tubes, machines and in an incubator to keep his temperature up. He was examined by the consultant every day, but after three days he shook his head and proclaimed the opinion that Jamie was not coming around as quickly as he had hoped. He said he was sorry, but this happened sometimes. Margaret and I were dumfounded, as we had not considered what problems could follow meningitis – all we had been praying for was his survival. There is a wrongly-held belief that meningitis is a 'brain disease', but it is not. It is inflammation of the meninges *around* the brain. Neither Margaret nor I could come to terms with the opinion of the consultant, and we still hoped for the best.

The following day after the consultation I visited as usual and Margaret was allowed to hold Jamie in her arms for the first time – tubes and all. He was very floppy, but she cradled him gently and as I walked into the room she looked up and told me she was certain he had attempted to smile at her. The doctor obviously did not believe what she was saying, and shook his head as he went out of the room. At that point Margaret handed him to me for a gentle cuddle, and as she spoke to him and smiled I saw what she meant – he *did* make a very weak attempt to smile at us. He was so weak, his eyes could not focus or stay still, he could not lift his limbs or suck a bottle very well or even hold his head up, but he definitely tried to smile.

Next day it was more apparent, and believe it or not within a week no one would have believed this baby had been about an hour from death so recently. His recovery was nothing but miraculous, and even the doctor was amazed. Jamie returned to the loveable nosey little rogue just as before so quickly, and was soon allowed to return home. He was kept on antibiotics for a considerable length of time but had obviously not suffered any apparent brain damage, and all that was noticeable from his ordeal was one scar from a large blister on his elbow. We believed he had escaped completely from after-effects, but during his later teenage and adult years there were some medical difficulties as a direct result of his illness. However, he was lucky to be alive at all; not so some other babies who had been in hospital with him at the same time. Jamie eventually married and became a father himself.

Our experience certainly brought home how difficult it is to diagnose meningitis, and certainly the doctor who had initially attended Jamie missed some obvious symptoms. He should have realised the pain and stiffness in the baby's joints and limbs, and the fontanelle which should have still been soft at four months was raised due to pressure inside the skull.

For the following year after Jamie's recovery everyone joined in doing all sorts of things to raise money for both Tameside and Pendlebury Hospitals by organising jumble sales, raffles and donations – anything we could think of, and at the end of the twelve months we handed cheques for £2,000 each to the hospitals concerned. Pendlebury spent their money on a new intensive care ward which would provide five more cots for sick babies, and we hoped so much that other little ones would be saved as a result of this.

I had realised during Jamie's illness that there were no support groups for meningitis victims and their relatives in our area whatsoever, so I set up a local group and ran it for five years from home in an evening, including telephone support. Through this we made many lasting friendships and heard some dreadful stories, but hopefully good came out of bad this time. Thankfully Jamie himself never knew what he had gone through, for which we were grateful.

After this dreadful period – albeit it having lasted only around three weeks in total (it had seemed like an eternity), the threads of communication were picked up once more with Vera, though we had kept her advised of the situation throughout.

It took some time to readjust after such a traumatic experience, and we watched little Jamie like a hawk but he thrived and returned to normality very quickly.

Ian suggested that he and I take our first holiday abroad and it was so refreshing to have something nice to look forward to now; neither of us had ever been out of England before – how exciting.

CHAPTER 9

New Places and Beginnings

———

After the trauma of Jamie's illness had settled down, Margaret had married and life seemed more stable. The young couple still lived with us, so Ian and I decided it was safe to go ahead and fly abroad. Helen would not be left alone at home and of course was still at college, so Ian's suggestion was that we visit Pompeii in southern Italy whilst staying in Sorrento. He knew that from childhood I had always been fascinated with the story of Pompeii being buried in time when Mount Vesuvius erupted in AD 79, and I suspect he thought it would be an offering I could not refuse to actually visit my childhood dream! I guess that was one way of getting me on an aircraft!

By now I believed I had Italian blood in me, so to visit the country of my birth father sounded incredible! Once we had experienced flying abroad there was to be no stopping us in the following ten years, during which we visited the Canary Islands, America, Austria, Crete, Egypt, Greece and Turkey. This first trip certainly started the longing to travel in me.

I shall never forget how it felt first landing on Italian soil. It really did feel like 'home' somehow; the atmosphere, food, climate, people and lifestyle. Everything just felt 'right'. It was a wonderful introduction to foreign travel staying in Sorrento, and a time I shall never forget. Always at the back of my mind was the information I had received about my birth father being Italian. How I wished I knew where in Italy his roots were, but of course it was not to be as I had no information whatsoever. Still, it was sufficient to realise I had achieved more than I had ever expected.

Ian, who was asthmatic, felt so well in the Italian sunshine. We had a really weird experience on the day we climbed to the top of Mount Vesuvius, for as we walked from the car park up to the crater we were just approaching the summit when there, walking towards us, was a work colleague who had left my office three years before to marry and move to London. This was unbelievable, and we could not guess what the odds were on unexpectedly meeting friends on the top of a volcano!

For twenty-seven years I had been corresponding with my penfriend Kathy, who lived in Cleveland, Ohio, USA. This, then, was another wonderful experience the following year as we flew over to America to visit them. Kathy had accompanied her mother and sister to visit us back in 1966 when I had just started work, and was not allowed any time off, and so I had not spent much time with them during their trip. This made it extra exciting to experience America for the first time and spend a wonderful holiday with Kathy and her family.

They took us to Sea World, of course, the McKinley Monument, Amish country and – for a treat – Kathy's mother, (Auntie Grace as I called her) booked Kathy, her husband Bob, Ian and I in at Niagara Falls for two nights before we returned home. Bob drove us from Ohio to Niagara (which took five hours), and to see the fabulous Niagara Falls was an experience never to be forgotten. I had purchased a camcorder for this holiday, and still have the footage of that wonderful trip.

We did visit our American friends once again in 1999, but this time we flew to Washington DC where Kathy, Bob and Auntie Grace met us and we spent two days exploring the capital. My friendship with Kathy, started when she was eight and I was nine, has now lasted a lifetime.

And so, after a little episode spread over a few years of

happy travel and experiences, we must now return to 1992 and pick up the original threads of the story, for at that time the 'old wooden spoon' was working overtime, stirring up a few storms ...

Baby Jamie's recovery had been nothing short of a miracle, and after our trip to Sorrento, Ian and I had returned with renewed vigour and positive feelings about the future. Still, nothing is ever perfect as something always seems to occur which prevents total happiness, and for the next few months I became very apprehensive about all four of our parents. Ian and I were both 'only' children, so of course the responsibility for their care came down to just the two of us.

Ian's parents were at that time being cared for in a residential home near my parents, who still lived in their own property close by. Our homelife consisted of Helen, Margaret, her husband and baby Jamie who celebrated his first milestone birthday in September 1990 – a celebration none of us had thought we would ever see!

Margaret had rather rushed into her marriage at the early age of nineteen, although her husband initially seemed a pleasant and genuine person. Thankfully our house was large enough to accommodate everyone comfortably, but within eleven months baby Rebekah was born and it was obvious the young couple needed to set up their own housekeeping. Our once-tiny family was now expanding!

Ian's mother, Dorothy – one of the most wonderful mother-in-laws anyone could have, became ill in 1992 and her memory was badly affected. She had always been supportive of Ian and I, and extremely understanding of how difficult my mum and Gran could be. Certainly my in-laws prevented a third world war breaking out many times during our marriage! How Dot loved jogging Becky on her knee, although she could not remember who the baby girl belonged to! She passed away in January 1993 just a month short of her ninetieth birthday. Until she turned eighty-six or eighty-seven

First time abroad. Sorrento and visit to Pompeii.

she had continuously ridden around Droylsden on her bicycle doing jobs for the 'elderly' – most of whom were much younger than herself, and she still played the organ in church every Sunday. She had also continued swimming three times a week.

We were very worried how Ian's dad, George, would cope when his wife became ill, but he took the situation reasonably well and seemed settled and happy enough with our visits and enjoying his great-grandson and little great-granddaughter.

It was around this time I became concerned about my own parents. Dad seemed to think he was doing the housework well, but it soon became obvious he was not hanging out freshly washed clothes – he only thought he was. He had two chip-pan fires. On one occasion he had rushed out into the garden with the flaming chip-pan, and it was a wonder he didn't get badly burnt. He was also vague about other matters. A neighbour across the road from my parents was also concerned, and she called in to see them every morning and then rang me at work to reassure me they were all right. I lived on a knife-edge every time the telephone rang, in case it was news to say the house had burnt down or that either Mum, Dad or both of them had suffered a serious accident. Mum never got out of her chair; she would give Dad instructions which he would automatically obey, and it was impossible to broach the subject of my concerns with Mum as she was completely in denial and greatly resented me implying that perhaps things were not quite right. When I shakily told her I felt Dad was not remembering things properly, her retort was simply that he had always had a bad memory, so I was up against a brick wall.

I was now in full-time employment, 9 a.m. to 5 p.m.., with great responsibility and an intense workload. Added to this was the situation at home, which was not perfect by any means, and my world seemed to revolve around keeping the peace at times. I guess my situation was much like that of many people – coping at a time of life between youngsters on the one hand, the elderly on the other etc., but unfortunately there was no one to share it with as Ian still worked permanent nights, getting up early afternoon and preparing to go to work again that evening. He did not have the time or capacity really to assist much with regard to my parents. Never one to manage coping with problems, he was very insecure outside of his safety zone of routine. That is how he was, so gentle, pleasant, and what I say is no sense of criticism whatsoever: he was the most truthful and honest person anyone could ever have met!

In March 1993 things came to a head, not long after Dorothy had died. Whilst visiting friends overnight we had a telephone call to say that Dad had gone 'walkabout' and Mum was in screaming hysterics. The journey home that day was terrible: my imagination running riot with what might have happened to Dad. Thankfully we discovered he had been found taking a walk up to our old house – at least that is where we believed he had been heading. He couldn't understand why Mum was in such a state. Being very concerned I approached their doctor with my concerns, but the only feedback from him was to say he had recently checked them for their blood pressures and could not detect anything wrong with Dad's capability of speech or understanding. So, another dead end!

I knew things were wrong. Very wrong. But how to get help? Unfortunately it took a crisis. Soon afterwards, therefore, I received a telephone call whilst at work from the local hospital to say *both* my parents had collapsed in the car park of the local Co-op whilst doing their usual little shopping trip! We never did discover who either fell or collapsed first but when one of our solicitors drove me up to the hospital, because I was too shaky and shocked to drive, I was told Mum wasn't too bad and was to be discharged, but Dad was to be kept in for a few days for tests.

Mum hated being on her own, so I took her back home with me for the night. It was then I realised just what Dad had been trying to cope with, even in his mixed-up state. She was up every half an hour shouting for me throughout the night, and then at 6.30 a.m., just after Ian got home and I had fallen asleep she was screaming at me it was time to get up! Margaret and her little family were in their own home by this time, but thankfully her husband, who was unemployed reassured me he would stay with Mum during the day whilst I was at work. However, she insisted on going to her own home to await Dad's discharge from hospital.

When I went to the hospital after work to collect Dad, the psychiatric consultant was most unhappy about things and told me he was arranging for Dad to attend day care three times a week so he could be observed. Nor was he happy about the fact of Dad having to take care of Mum, so he arranged for her, too, to attend a different day centre whilst Dad was out. Of course it didn't work – there was no way Mum was going anywhere, especially with strangers around. So, on the first day Dad was back at home she cancelled their taxis, cancelled both day care centres, Meals on Wheels and a laundry service, which had also been arranged. And that was that! No one was going to tell my mum what she could or couldn't do!

The following Sunday Mum had a fall and told Dad to call me, which he did. When Margaret and I arrived Dad was in the garden tending his beautiful yellow roses and looked up in surprise when we drew up in the car. He had forgotten everything which had happened. What a sight confronted us when we went inside – Mum had fallen onto the rim of the electric fire, which thankfully was not on at the time. Margaret had to take the two small children out of the room immediately as Mum's tablets were strewn everywhere – on her lap, down the side of the chair and all over the floor. I rang for an ambulance as she was obviously very disorientated and rambling, but it took two ambulances and in the end a police constable to give the second ambulance men permission to take her to hospital as she was refusing to go. To this day I can hear her screams as they took her out to the ambulance that day, but we discovered later she had been only two hours away from death with kidney failure!

During the three months Mum was in hospital, a long way from us in Withington the other side of Manchester, Dad spent a lot of time with us but would not stay away from home overnight. On his own he was perfectly amiable about day care, which he thoroughly enjoyed as there were tea dances, singing and entertainment. When I collected him after work, he had a meal with us and we put old films on which he remembered, and took him for rides in the countryside at weekends. When I took him home at bedtime he took his medications and was fine until morning. He was an absolute delight in that time, for which I am so grateful. The only downside was that I had to sell his car, as he kept putting it out on his driveway ready to take a trip somewhere. It was far too dangerous to allow him to do such a thing, but he never forgave me or understood why I had to do this.

We visited Mum every other evening due to the distance,

which was a nightmare for me as the moment I set foot in the ward she would berate and interrogate me, and obviously she detested me because I had been the cause of her having been taken into hospital! After a couple of weeks of this I collapsed in tears and the ward sister demanded to know why. She was very understanding and reassuring, which helped a lot.

There was no spell of light relief or happiness during this time, as whilst Dad was attending day care he was diagnosed with the early stages of Alzheimer's Disease, which was not going to improve. Doctor Oliver was lovely and wished to put a Guardianship Order on Dad for his protection, but unfortunately Mum was due to return home and because she was considered 'compos mentis' the psychiatrist had no authority to prevent him going back. He told me that if Dad returned home to Mum it would be 'disastrous' – and unfortunately this turned out to be the case.

When Mum returned home the house had to be changed around, with her sleeping downstairs in the dining room and with other facilities put in place downstairs. It did not take me long to realise Dad was no longer sleeping upstairs either – he was simply snoozing on the settee so he could hear her should she need him. During the day he would fall asleep and she would prod him awake with her walking stick and sometimes push the coffee table into his legs to wake him up and make a cup of tea. His legs were always bruised. The state of the house deteriorated rapidly. When I attempted to do something, Dad – my gentle, calm Dad – began to get irate, saying he had 'done it', though he couldn't remember what he needed to do, or what had been done. Social services visited on my request, but of course Mum gave Dad instructions to make a drink or do things whilst they were there and he followed her instructions mechanically, so they did not realise how bad he was or their true situation. Mum told them she did a lot of things to help when, in effect, she did nothing. I believe she was frightened, as she hated change, and I understood this. I tried hard to talk to her and explain but she still stuck to her guns in denial that anything was wrong. In the end I wrote a five-page letter to social services telling them everything that had been happening, and thankfully they agreed to make a further visit.

It was now September and the situation had turned into hell. Every day from midnight to midnight I was terrified something unspeakable would happen, and there were family problems too, as Margaret was pregnant again and unwell. Her husband could be volatile and quite nasty by this time. Thankfully, at least we managed to give Helen an eighteenth birthday party. That was the only pleasant time.

A new head of department had joined social services when my letter was received and she agreed to go round and assess the situation for herself. What a relief, as prior to this I knew I had not been believed as to how volatile and vulnerable my parents had become. Of course the problem arose as to how the social workers would get access into the house, as if callers came to the front door Mum would tell Dad to hide in the kitchen until they went away. The wonderful neighbour, who called in every morning, helped out here as she stayed until the social workers arrived, and she let them in that day. They agreed and were totally satisfied that Mum and Dad were high risk from what they saw, but the problem still remained that whatever was 'put into place' would be cancelled immediately by Mum.

It was too late. Just a week after social services had seen the situation for themselves, on the 19th of December, I realised Dad was quite ill and had jaundice. His doctor requested a consultant to visit and I stayed off work during his visit. He immediately sent Dad into hospital, telling me he was very ill indeed, and he sent Mum into a care home on a temporary basis, telling me she was 'senile' and if she prevented Dad getting the treatment he needed he would section her! I would have hated that, and thankfully with assistance from other people she did comply, under great protest.

Without going into more detail, they were both given places at a care home the following January after Dad had been given a small 'repair' operation, but we knew his condition was terminal. I did not want them to be split up and thankfully they went to the same residential home, but in their own rooms. It was a sad Christmas and impossible to explain things to Mum, who still denied anything was wrong with Dad. They were eighty-one and eighty-three at this time, and just a month short of their sixtieth wedding anniversary.

Dad soon settled at 'Holme Lea' with no problem, as he was not aware of his situation and a lot of his memories were from the past. He seemed to know me but could not remember my name. He was so sweet, friendly and his wonderful self with the staff, which soon made them care a great deal for him, and he thoroughly enjoyed the tea dances, entertainment and singing provided for the residents. He even got up on the stage and sang, having a lovely tenor voice. Margaret was able to take the children to see him and they would play in the big conservatory – Jamie was now five, Becky two and a half, and Margaret was expecting a new baby. Dad always had sweeties in his pocket for the children and he would watch them play, but if they had little tantrums he started to get upset with them, so we had to be a little careful. He always loved children, and should have had a large family of his own really!

Mum never settled at Holme Lea' – I realised later she had been suffering mini strokes, and was in and out of hospital from the first day. On Mothering Sunday that year I had just had a bad dose of flu and was not allowed to go into the hospital, so I had telephoned each day but was a bit concerned about some things I was told about Mum being rather delusional. I returned to work on the 28th of March 1994, the day Mum was to be discharged back to 'Holme Lea', and requested the nurse when I telephoned that morning to tell Mum I would see her later in the afternoon. It was not to be. By 1 p.m. we had received an urgent request to go to the hospital immediately, but she had died unexpectedly. My dad died just seven weeks later – I will never know if he realised it was Mum's funeral he had attended, but just three days beforehand he had turned to a lady sitting next to him and said, 'This is my daughter, Judith'. Nature can be so strange at times!

And so, life was about to change yet again, but there were some unexpected results with Vera and so many unexplained questions.

CHAPTER 10

More Changes

It took quite a long time to recover from the difficulties of the past two years, and Mum's death had been a dreadful shock, as we had expected her to outlive Dad. As I sat at her bedside, my mind was a maelstrom of feelings and thoughts. She looked so tiny and birdlike, so vulnerable and frail. Why, oh why, had I always been so frightened of her? She had never abused me physically, and considering I was much taller than Mum it had been strange just how much she had mentally dominated and controlled me. From early childhood Mum and Gran's word had been absolute law, and even when Gran died that regime was still with me concerning Mum. I had never even contemplated thwarting her wishes, rules or commands. Always I had acceded to her discipline and it never, even at the age of forty-six, occurred to me to go against her wishes. This was the main reason I had found it so hard to sort things out for her when she needed that help – I was scared of telling her anything!

I have never understood the strength of her hold over me or what, indeed, she could have actually done to me if I had rebelled. It was so ingrained in me to simply accept without question and was a matter of conscience that had dominated my entire life thus far. And now she had gone. There was no feeling of relief or freedom – just terrible sadness that my mum had been so insecure and frightened of life. It had affected everyone, my dad, myself and most of her married life too. I could put this down to wartime experiences, as it is beyond me how anyone coped with those dark years. She herself was also obviously extremely dominated by her mother, my gran.

But on the other hand, where would I have ended up without her and Gran? They had been the two people (so far as I knew back then) who had been instrumental in taking me out of 'somewhere' as a baby. I had a warm and secure home, although I always hated leaving its enfolding fortress to go out to school where the Big Unknown World did not really like me. The odd girl; the lonely shy girl; the girl who was completely ruled without a mind of her own. None of that mattered, for at home my world was happy, despite most of it being pretend and unwordly. I knew Dad would have given my mum a wonderful life if she had only given him the chance, but instead she had unwittingly curtailed his chances and tied him into a fairly lonely existence for nearly sixty years.

Dad was a staunch believer in 'duty' and he once told me that around six months after they had married there were concerns as he felt he had not married just my mum, but both Mum and Gran. He never came 'first' with Mum. He had gone to see his own father for some advice, who had told him, 'Eh, lad thy's med thy bed and thy must lie on it.' And he did, because of his 'duty'. I know Mum and Gran never became close to my dad's parents and family, and he never told me much about them. All he said was that they considered he had 'married above his station' and therefore did not like to visit. He did tell me once that when his own mother was dying in hospital he was told to ask the 'two women' who had visited her not to return again. Goodness knows what they had said or done!

The saddest thing of all regarding my mum is that I realise I never, in all those years, had an 'adult' conversation with her. I was 'told'. Always. So many of my friends had such a wonderful bond with their mothers, and how I would have loved our relationship to be like that. We missed such a lot.

It might be considered at this point that the old wooden spoon would stop stirring for some time, but it was not to be. Ian's dad, George, unexpectedly died in his sleep the following December, and so that meant we had lost all four of our parents within a two-year period. We were so glad George had lived long enough to welcome Margaret's new baby, Liam, who was born that September. We will always remember his gentle face as he cradled the new baby and stroked his great-granddaughter Becky's hair. George and Dorothy had been advised not to have more children after Ian was born, and my father-in-law always told me I was the daughter he had never had. How wonderful to have given him our two daughters, and now a great-granddaughter and two great-grandsons!

I have to admit that following the loss of Mum and Dad, sorting all the legalities out was done in a sort of trance, and perhaps having a full-time job was the best thing, putting my mind on the positive now instead of the negative.

We had not forgotten Vera during the past couple of years and kept in touch by telephone, but we had not seen anything of her properly. Of course we were now free to bring Vera to our home for a visit, and she came a few times, but the loss of my parents had another strange effect on this situation.

Up until their deaths, Vera had been so nice. She was always generous but did not offer information. We had got on so well and visited her as and when possible. She loved the girls and her great-grandchildren, and on numerous occasions we had sat and talked whilst I had attempted to find out whatever I could about my own history but this was fairly sparse and nothing new was added. She did not elaborate a great deal, and of course had closed a door on many of her difficult and sad memories, but I had learnt I had to try and separate the real from the imaginary at times.

There was now also the freedom and opportunity to meet more of my birth family, and on a trip to Chester Vera took me to meet my three uncles and their families; so many cousins, aunts and uncles it was impossible to remember all of their names. I became closest to my uncles. All three of them were such lovely men – Eric, Donald and Albert. We spoke to each other regularly by telephone, but sadly not too long after our meetings both Don and Albert died. Still, it had been beyond my wildest dreams to even meet people who were blood relatives, and I have always been so thankful since that time to have known these very special people.

I really expected Vera to become part of our little family now, although I still had stirrings of guilt in my heart, but I knew no one would get hurt by her visits and involvement any more. Alas, it was not to be.

Vera was to turn sixty-five in July 1994, and as always I posted a birthday card and gift to her. From the time of my first meeting with my birth mother we had continued a friendly relationship whereby I had always used her Christian name by which to call her. My daughters always called her 'Vera' too, but Margaret's children called her 'Nanna Vera'. She understood this, or appeared to, so I was greatly surprised on Vera's birthday when she telephoned me at work and said she had not received a birthday gift or card. Nonplussed I simply replied that the post was probably late, but then she made a statement which gave her away, in which she told me, 'You haven't called me "Mother".'

I stood there, not taking in what she was saying. Had she received my parcel or not? Obviously she had, and was stating something she was unhappy with. I asked her what she meant, because I had never used the word 'Mother' – she had always told me she understood that I could not replace the only mother I had actually known. So I gently reminded her it was not yet four months since I had lost both my parents. At this point I started to shake and tremble, but she retorted, 'Oh forget them – they've gone now.' Had she grown a different head?

Even though I had always been non-confrontational I could not cope with this statement, and was most definitely not going to have *anyone* telling me to forget my Mum and Dad. This was bang out of order. Whatever I felt were difficult situations in the past and that I had never felt truly close to my mum, my parents were still the ones who had brought me up and nurtured me, not to mention what they had possibly rescued me from had I not been in their care! Vera had always displayed great thankfulness to the people who had taken me and kept me safe, and now she was trying to turn the situation around. Standing there, holding the telephone, it was quite a shock. I just told Vera I was very busy at work and would telephone her later on that evening to discuss the matter further. She slammed the telephone down on me and would not answer it when I did call her later that evening. After a couple of days' silence and refusal to speak to me I concluded she was throwing her toys out of the pram, figuratively speaking, and that she wished me to now 'replace' my mum with her, which was impossible.

I guess this is the fear of most adoptive parents when their children set out to find their birth parents. However, the children themselves rarely wish to replace anyone, searching for birth parents is simply a search for themselves, to know the reasons behind their fostering or adoption, to find out just who they are, where they came from and their heritage. So, it was hard now to believe that someone who had been so friendly and – I thought – understanding, had turned the tables on me after five years. Why? What made her change at this time? We had reached a period when our friendship could develop and I felt so guilty and wondered if it was justice for deceiving my parents by going behind their backs a few years before? Now I felt that I might have actually opened Pandora's Box without realising it!

Thankfully at this point I was still in touch with Vera's younger sister, Betty, and also Uncles Eric and Don. I therefore wrote a long letter to Vera first of all, telling her how sorry I was that she felt unable to speak to me after the loss of my parents but stressing that our door would always be open to her should she feel she wished to become part of the family openly and above board. She never replied.

I sent copies of that letter to Auntie Betty, Uncle Eric and Uncle Don, knowing now how Vera could twist a story, and I was very concerned that they knew the truth and what I had said to Vera. I wished them to know I had in no way been cruel or nasty with Vera, but that I could not accede to what she obviously wished. I had realised some time before that Vera was capable of prevarication when explaining things, and did not wish my aunt or uncles to feel I had in any way been conducive in causing her grief or pain. They were both very understanding, and Betty told me once more that Vera could be difficult when she didn't get her own way, and that she frequently could 'change the goalposts' when it suited her. I understood now what Betty meant, and that Vera could be extremely manipulative in order to get her own way. My letter to Vera had only contained the reasons I was not going to change my opinion regarding my parents, and hoped she would reconsider her refusal to speak to me. Unfortunately I never heard from her again, and for the next two years the only news I had of Vera was from Betty.

It was such a shame, as those two years could have been so full for Vera with new great-grandchildren, visiting, meeting friends etc., but instead she chose to cut herself off, quite literally, and she became quite a recluse. Betty visited her sister of course from time to time, and attended when Vera was ill or taken to hospital for one reason or another, and the social workers who attended Vera on a daily basis had a very difficult time with her I believe. Certainly the daily records left by her carers told the story without any nonsense, and she had not allowed them to assist in looking after herself. It was a tragedy and completely unnecessary.

Sadly, Vera died of a heart attack on the 19th of July 1996 at the age of sixty-eight. This was a very sad time for all of us, but she had made her own choices and it would not have been right to accede to dictatorship. I did attend Vera's funeral, along with Auntie Betty, Uncle Don and Uncle Eric, which was quite a surreal experience, but although Uncle Don died soon after I kept in touch with Uncle Eric and Auntie Betty, and strangely enough in later years found myself living not too far away from Auntie Betty!

And so the latter years of the 1990s trundled on with a lot of changes, the usual run of problems, some lovely holidays but the ever-present undercurrent of things being 'stirred up'. I was going through a phase which was impossible to describe. It was a feeling of being lost, alone, unable to help where I would have liked to, but frequently was not permitted. I had to stand back and see events and situations unfurl, but there is only so much one can do. Vera was no longer in our lives, and I knew that eventually I would probably make an attempt to put together some more of the 'jigsaw puzzle' surrounding my own life, although at that time it felt I would never progress. How to discover further information? How to move on now, for there was no one to ask?

There were, however, two strange things that happened after my mum died. Mum and Gran must have possessed papers relating to myself and their long-term fostering of me, but although I suspect these were locked in a compartment in our dining room bureau, this compartment was open and empty after I turned eighteen. They must have destroyed anything to prevent me from reading papers relating to my fostering.

The first odd thing was that in Mum's tiny handbag diary there were two handwritten items. One was a poem about 'children who were adopted', and the first time I saw this item I began to wonder if, in fact, Mum and Gran had ever met Vera and attended the family home at Saighton or Crewe, wherever it was. This was weird, as Vera had a copy of that very poem framed on her lounge wall! Most peculiar. Had the two matriarchs, when they were deciding whether to take me on or not, been to 'check out' my family 'stock'? This was very important to Gran, whenever she spoke about peoples' past history or families in general. She liked to know what sort of family people 'came from', and would most definitely not have considered taking on a child into her family she would have considered of 'unsuitable stock'. I know this sounds ridiculous in this day and age, but that was her way of thinking – most definitely. Sadly the question about this verse will never be answered as I unfortunately threw that little diary away and I have never been able to find another copy. If someone else in the family had taken the framed verse from Vera's flat after her death perhaps it is still in existence, but I have no way of finding out. Maybe it was simply coincidence. If Mum and Gran had not visited Vera's family home then where did Mum get the words from? Very odd. Another option which occurred to me was whether my situation had been a 'private adoption'; in other words, had they known my real mother and grandparents? When there is absolutely no knowledge the mind makes up all sorts of possibilities and stories.

The second strange item was a list on blue paper, containing a little bit of information about me. It read:

'Judith Mary Boothman Ashton'.
Born 16th February 1948.
First address 89 North Road, Wolverhampton OQA.
Registered 10th March 1948.
Second Address 4 Wilton Street, Wallasey, L.D.A. 11th May 1948
Third Address Kilrie Home, Northwich Road, Knutsford LFF.
October 1948.
Fourth Address 75 Castleway, Pendleton, Salford 6, Lancs. NPA.
June 16th 1949.
Fifth Address 36 Town Lane, Charlesworth, Derbyshire, via Manchester
July 23rd 1950.

Judith Mary Ashton Boothman
Born 16ᵗ February 1948.
1ˢᵗ address. 89 North Road.
Wolverhampton. O.g.A.
Registered 10ᵗ March 1948.
2ⁿᵈ Address, 4. Wilton Street.
Wallasey L.D.A.
11ᵗ May 1948
3ʳᵈ Address. Kilric Home
Northwich Road
Knutsford. L.D.A.
Oct 8ᵗ 1948.
4ᵗ address. 75 Castleway
Pendleton
Salford 6.
June 16ᵗ 1949. Lancs. Ni
5ᵗ address. 36 Town Lane
Charlesworth.
Derbyshire
nr manchester
1ˢᵗ A.

The elusive piece of blue paper!

113

This small piece of paper was carefully put away by me after my mum died, but sadly in the weeks following Mum's loss, with Dad's death seven weeks later, perhaps I was not as careful with it as I should have been, and for quite a few years I thought I had lost it. This seemed to be the only link which would enable me to move ahead with the searches I so wished to carry out.

Work took up the majority of my life and was not easy. I was handling clients' personal matters and was more or less put in charge when my boss went on holiday. Huge amounts of money exchanged hands when property sales and purchases were completed, and I fretted a lot over the responsibilities during those times. Perhaps all this mental preoccupation did help in a strange way by reducing thoughts of what had happened, but it was almost like being a zombie, automatically carrying out necessary jobs, work, and always exhausted. I had not lost interest in tracing my roots of course, but losing that bit of blue paper seemed to be the worst thing of all. Had I carelessly thrown away the final and most informative link so far in my story?

As Vera actually died in 1996 there is another situation to record, although this is a little out of 'sequence', but a huge step in my search for 'lost family', which took place in 1995. I had no contact with Vera from 1994, because she cut me off as I would not do as she wished, and as already noted she had made it difficult sometimes for me to verify what I was told.

At our first meeting she had advised me I had two half-siblings called Robert and Carolyn, who were born in Ireland when she was married. Vera's story was that there was a house fire in which her husband and children had died, so of course I was very upset for her terrible tragedy and all of my family's hearts went out to Vera for the five years she was part of our lives. She would not talk about it very much, of course, so I did not push for information in case I upset her any further.

114

One or two things Vera told me did not ring true or make sense. I tried to find out more about this tragic event, but how to discover the truth was difficult. Obviously such a disaster would have been a front-page story in such a small community where Vera had been living, so there should have been some record. I telephoned a local newspaper in the Cookstown area of Northern Ireland where Vera had told me this all happened. A lovely girl at the newspaper was very interested and actually went through three years of microfiche film in an attempt to find newspaper coverage of the incident. Nothing was discovered at all. Strange.

Vera had told me the children were born in 1957 and 1959, so the next step was to acquire their birth certificates, and these were readily available. However, there were no death certificates and I realised my half-brother and half-sister could still be alive.

It was impossible to tell Vera what I thought I had discovered, for she would no longer speak to me by then. I have never understood why she told me such an outrageous and untrue story unless she herself had been told this by someone else, which didn't seem likely. I could only think that, because of situations no one knows anything about, she simply had to 'close a door' on her past. Perhaps more would come to light in the future?

Discovering further information was difficult, but as I knew Vera had lived in Cookstown during her marriage I decided to place an advertisement anonymously in the local paper requesting information from anyone who knew my siblings. It was not too long before I received a reply from Carolyn through a private box number, and after quite a few telephone conversations I discovered there was another side to the story other than Vera's synopsis.

So I knew I had a half-sister whom I was speaking to! Another unbelievable event, and Carolyn and I could not wait to meet each other.

Ian had wished to travel through Ireland for many years, so we now took the opportunity to tour parts of Ireland in 1995 and an arrangement was made to meet Carolyn and my half-brother Robert at the end of the trip. We took our car across to Ireland and drove to Mitcheltown first of all in southern Ireland, and then made our way during the week up through Galway to Cookstown where Carolyn kindly accommodated us for two nights. It was an odd feeling to meet her for the first time, but we could not have been made more welcome, and we were very well looked after. Obviously we chattered away for hours, and my half-sister was as amazed as I was at the discoveries, as she had never had any knowledge of my existence, either! We did look very similar to each other. We also met Robert, who seemed very nice, but I felt Carolyn was holding back a little regarding him and was rather nervous at our meeting him.

The most amazing place we visited whilst there was the Giant's Causeway as during our two days with Carolyn we went out and about and it was lovely to share that time with my newly-found sister and her two little girls – my nieces! I still have the video film of Ian holding the children's hands as they scrambled over the giant stones.

Now we had a different story to hear. Robert and Carolyn had been brought up by their father's sister, whom Carolyn called 'Mammy'. She was a lovely lady and it was good to meet her. Mammy told us that Vera had actually walked out on her two young children when Robert was around three years old and Carolyn just a young baby of a few months. There were different opinions as to why this had been the case and her reasons, but there did not appear to be any justification, and it is something of a mystery to know where Vera went at that time and, indeed, if it was with someone else. She certainly returned to England at some point. One cannot make judgements without both sides of a story, but a few pieces of the 'life jigsaw' were beginning to take their place.

Carolyn and Robert were brought up by Mammy and their father, but none of us could come to terms with why Vera had told such a dreadful story about the children's fake deaths. Certainly as I had grown to know Vera better it was obvious that after the horrendous fire accident when she was only fourteen or fifteen, followed by my birth when I was apparently taken away from her, she was never quite the same. This is understandable, but her inability to reveal the truth at times made it more difficult to dig out what was and was not correct. Still, I was in any event discovering far more than I had ever thought possible at that time, and now had a half-brother and a half-sister. Wow. I was the eldest of *three* children!

I have kept in touch with Carolyn, who is lovely, but sadly Robert took advantage of us to come over to England a couple of years later, and when he did so there were unbelievable problems and difficulties caused by the untruths he fabricated. Therefore, when we moved house early in the millennium, although we felt sorry for Carolyn, we did not advise her at that time of our whereabouts as we did not wish Robert to put pressure on her to reveal our new address. We definitely did not wish him to turn up unannounced on the doorstep. Perhaps it was for the best at that time, but thankfully some years later Carolyn and I renewed our friendship and sistership, which has continued.

How life twists and turns with events, people and places. I had made a major step of progress in discovering my half-siblings, but on the other hand even more questions were arising and in the years before and after the millennium it seemed impossible to imagine I would ever discover anything else.

How wrong could one be?

CHAPTER 11

The Millennium is in Sight

———

What a wonderful experience to witness the beginning of a new millennium. I will never forget the celebrations with peoples' hopes and dreams for the forthcoming century. We were invited to join neighbours for this wonderful event and thankfully nothing dreadful happened to computers despite dire warnings!

After the previous years' trials and tribulations life seemed to fall very flat. I guess it was also a time of grieving for all four of our parents, with the added problems of sorting many things out. This always takes a long time, but of course big changes occurred at home, too. Helen was now in her early twenties and courting, working hard and was always a very independent young woman. She had gone through tribulations with the rest of the family regarding very difficult times and I feel she missed out on a lot during her teenage years. She had never complained and bore the rest of the family's troubles in a stalwart manner. When she was born, it was said she seemed to have been born 'grown up' – always a sensible head, a mind of her own and the ability to know what was right and wrong without being told. She was most definitely not going to follow her sister's difficult pathway and could really stand up for herself when necessary.

Margaret, in the meantime, was struggling along with her family of three young children after a marriage which had been doomed from the start. It was hard to see what was happening and of course we helped when allowed to do so, but despite them moving to a better house she was inevitably left alone in a situation she simply couldn't cope with. She did her best and that is all anyone can do. The children were never neglected but their happiness came at the price of her health and peace of mind for many years.

Ian and I were now rattling around in an empty house. Ian was happy enough with his night-shifts.; his free hours during the day before preparing for work were spent in his beloved garden or attempting to help Margaret out where he could. He began taking his grandsons on country walks or to play golf at various parks in the area, which they loved as they grew a bit older.

I was very restless though at that time, and spent most evenings alone unless a friend called round. With having one car between us Ian took it to his night-shift with him so I could not go very far in an evening, and was tired after the stresses at work. After the necessary housework I was too weary to be bothered about much. Being alone was not really the problem as I had always been used to solitary occupations, and I guess at this time I was able to resurrect some hobbies and of course the Meningitis Trust Group I ran together with an evening telephone helpline also filled in some space. However, loneliness and depression are not good housemates! Having extended family would have assisted at this time but we were back to a very small group and friends had their own families and worries to cope with.

Looking back, I think a lot of the problem was 'empty nest' syndrome, which nearly all mothers experience when their chicks fly away. It would have been better if I had known my eldest daughter was happy, but I knew she wasn't until she remarried.

Helen had married prior to the millennium and she seemed settled. She and her fiancé had flown out to Barbados to marry, but sadly Ian and I could not go as we had already pre-booked a trip to America to visit our friends in Ohio once more and we could not have afforded it. However, she brought a beautiful video of the wedding home and we held receptions with both sets of parents on their return. The couple settled in a beautiful house not too far away and seemed very happy.

During those days I couldn't help wondering more about the past and just where I had come from. I had no answers, had no idea why I felt so out of place, and just didn't know where to go next regarding the discovery of further birth family information. How to move forward for more knowledge? There were so many questions without answers or even the likelihood of answers. Had the internet been part of our lives at that time it would have been wonderful, as information would have been more freely available. There were no television programmes either such as came later which explained how to trace lost families or even have the right to know about such things. It seemed to be a dead end. I cannot help feeling that not only myself but possibly thousands of people missed out because of this – certainly I was to discover much later in life what I had missed!

I had loved our visit to Italy some years before, and so when Ian suggested a Mediterranean cruise to cheer us up I thought it was a wonderful idea and we managed to save sufficiently to do this. Neither of us had ever been on a cruise before, and so Ian decided to sort one out for us! We both seemed to be good sailors so had no qualms about being on the sea.

And so the millennium gave to Ian and I the experience of our first 'cruise' holiday. The ship was a small Italian family-owned vessel called the *SS Monteray* and the trip was for nine days. She was launched in October 1931 and only took 701 passengers – a far cry from the 3,000 to 5,000 on today's liners! We would join the ship in Naples with an itinerary which took in Pompeii, Cairo, Rhodes, Ephesus, Kusadi, Piraeus and Athens with a few days in between. The Egyptian

Our Silver Wedding, 6th June ,1995.

section took in a trip to see the pyramids of course – something I had never expected to see in person. We were full of anticipation for this cruise, but even on that holiday trouble was brewing (or stirring!).

Although the *Monteray* was very small compared to modern cruisers, to us she seemed enormous. We had a very pleasant central cabin (no porthole windows) but unfortunately the bunk beds which folded down from the walls were extremely high on either side of the room and a step had to be used in order to get into them! I found this quite amusing as, after all, very little time was spent in the cabin when there was so much to see and do with the ship's entertainment and the wonderful day trips, but I soon changed my tune the next day!

Our en-suite was very tiny and on the second morning whilst getting dressed I leant on what I thought was the wall – however the tiny corner shower cubicle had a white curtain drawn across it (which merged it into the actual walls) and instead of leaning on a solid surface I fell backwards into the shower and was completely stunned. I was alone, as Ian had gone for an early morning swim, so when I came round I discovered I had banged my lower hip and back on the soap containers which were suspended on a floor to ceiling pole, and the edge of the shower rim had dug into my back. I was probably unconscious for a short time, but I had never seen a bruise like the one that rapidly developed on my back, and attempting to get up was excruciating. I had to wait for Ian to return to help me but when we managed to get down to the ship's doctor he pronounced I had cracked two ribs. There was no treatment, but he reassured me it would clear up in eight days or so. In actual fact it took eight weeks! Breathing was hard and so was walking, but I was so determined to visit those pyramids I would have gone on my knees if necessary!

So, it was a matter of grinning and bearing it. I had to walk slowly, try not to twist or bend, or be pulled up from a sitting position, but even lying on a sunbed was impossible as I could not get up without rolling onto the floor and then attempting to get up on my knees. Anyone who has had cracked ribs will know exactly how it was – not an experience I would be willing to repeat!

The worst thing of all was those bunk beds! We could not get a change of cabin as the ship was full (we were told), so it was a monumental task to negotiate onto a small stool and once up there I could not lean back on pillows as there was a gap between the end of the bunk bed and the wall, so there was nowhere to even prop a pillow!

I have to say that our fellow passengers on the ship were fantastic. They would prepare a cushioned area for me in the afternoon tea area and someone was always willing to lend a hand to pull me up when needed. Despite the disaster we both found the cruise fabulous and the places we visited were really wonderful. We hoped to take further cruises in the forthcoming years, but sadly this was not to be the case.

The only disappointment to me on the cruise (apart from my painful injury, that is) was that one of the 'land' trips had been to the Holy Land, which included a visit to the Church of the Nativity in Bethlehem. How I had looked forward to that, as it is somewhere I have always wished to visit, but it was not to be, as there were so many military troubles at the time our ship bypassed the venue completely and took us to Turkey instead. It was still very interesting but rather disappointing for me – still, with the pain I was experiencing it would have been difficult in any event.

Our holiday had been very therapeutic despite the ribs, so when we returned home it made us think that perhaps we should downsize now the girls had moved out and we didn't really need a four-bedroomed house any more. It was a shame because we really loved the property, but the decision was made and the house put up for sale. It took well over a year to sell as two prospective buyers fell through due to either lack of money in one case or a divorce with the other couple, but eventually things went ahead.

With our dear old computer 'brain' once more, how often do we wish in 'real life' that, like the computer, we could return to 'saved' information and bring it upon our screens again? How wonderful it would be if we could, in fact, return to previous years and 'restart' from that point. Impossible of course, but there is probably not one person alive who hasn't, at some time, felt this way.

For myself, looking back, if we had not moved maybe we could have re-housed Margaret and her three children instead of disposing of that house. She may not have wanted to come back to live with her parents, but it is something which I have often wondered might have made her life easier and filled ours. However, we cannot live our lives through our children, and so it was never even suggested.

Eventually we received a call from our estate agent to say that another offer had been put in for our house, and this time it went ahead so it was all systems go. My new home was a lovely little two-bedroom stone cottage with a 75-foot garden which had not been attended to for fifteen years, so the neighbours revealed. I have never seen such big stinging nettles in my life as those we discovered. Over the next few years that garden was completely remodelled and turned out to be a pride and joy.

In 2002 Ian was sixty-two, but despite having the opportunity to retire at sixty, having worked for the post office for forty years, he decided to carry on until sixty-five so long as his health remained stable. Apart from being asthmatic, which he seemed to know how to control well, he was quite happy. His lifelong wish had been to build a model train layout, and as the Hornby rolling stock and engines were expensive he wanted to purchase all those items whilst he was still working and could afford them as a hobby for his retirement years. A special board was affixed to the wall in the back bedroom and between us we began to put together the longed-for model. Ian bought the models and I made some scenery, which turned out to be a beautiful layout. We began this setup in 2003 and our young grandchildren were fascinated with it, of course. Little Liam in particular adored the Flying Scot, which had miniature lamps on the railway carriage tables which lit up – Ian would turn the central room light off and it was absolutely entrancing to see the little train going around the track with its little lamps in the carriage windows!

Ian was never a 'social' person. He was an only child, like myself, born in December 1939 just as the Second World War had broken out. Eight years my senior, he was twenty-eight when we met, thirty when we married, and he had never had a serious girlfriend before. Due to my rather restrictive life in childhood and teenage years I, too, of course, never had a social life and, as explained earlier, we had been penfriends. He was unable to communicate terribly well with his stammering or converse with people he did not know, so of course being in the Penfriend Society had been the most comfortable way for him to make friends.

This was not to say, in any way, that Ian had no emotion. He certainly did. I remember the pride, tenderness and caring in his face on the day we got married, vividly, the love, emotion and tears in his eyes each time he saw his newborn daughters, together with the love and concern for all four of our parents. But Ian could not ever transfer that emotion as, like my parents and gran, he was not tactile and was dreadfully (even painfully) shy – even in private – to convey his deepest feelings. Nor could he cope with problems, as I found out in the thirty-six years we shared, but would 'hide his head in the sand' because he simply could not cope with them.

By the time we married, when Ian was thirty, he was quite set in his ways, fiercely independent and happy with his own company. Therefore his work with the post office suited him very well. He had started off as an 'indoor' postman sorting letters, and apparently held the record in Newton Street, Manchester, GPO Sorting Office as being the postie who could sort most letters per minute! A hard worker, a wonderful husband, father and provider. He was not a selfish person in any way, shape or form, but just kept his emotions and dislikes to himself and could not share his innermost thoughts. A wonderful sense of humour and a peace-maker: he needed to be, with a mother-in-law like my mum, bless his heart!

Holidays, or rather booking them to suit both of us, was always a problem with the GPO. Ian was 'given' his three yearly sets of dates and had to adhere to them. On the other hand, my boss would not allow me to take holidays when *he* was away as I had to be his personal assistant at those times. This caused quite a bit of conflict, as the only way Ian could change his dates was if one of the other posties would swap with him, which sometimes was not possible. It did make things difficult from time to time but we seemed to survive these difficulties and had lots of lovely trips.

Helen's little daughter, Jessica, was born in 2001, so now we had four beautiful grandchildren who were the light of Ian's life. He was really looking forward to retiring when he reached sixty-five in 2005 as there would be a great deal to keep him busy and active.

We made plans for plenty of hill and mountain walking in the Lake District once he had plenty of free time – taking weekend breaks up there were first on his list, then of course there was our model train layout and all the other visits to places at home and abroad to look forward to. He had purchased quite a lot of 00 gauge rolling stock for the model train set.

From time to time we talked about Vera of course, and Ian was always trying to think how we could move ahead to discover more. We had kept in touch by phone with Auntie Betty, and once we did drive down to Tipton in the West Midlands to visit her when my half-brother Robert from Ireland was visiting us. This was before he caused all the problems, but sadly after we asked him to leave our home he turned up at Auntie Betty's expecting *her* to take him in. Thankfully she didn't!

And so our lives continued in this way and we were content. Margaret eventually remarried a much nicer person, and in 2002 little Harry joined her rapidly growing family. It was nice to see her in such an improved situation. Life was happy enough at this point, with days full of work, interest, travelling and companionship. However, it is a good job none of us know what is 'around the corner' and fate, wooden spoons or whatever obviously thought that six or seven years' peace and quiet was far too long ...

CHAPTER 12

The Unexpected ...

———

At the end of February 2004 my close friend Beryl was desperate to have a holiday. Her husband, Ben, a farmer, did not wish to go away at that time and leave the farm, so Beryl had found a good deal for a trip to Morocco. She told me she had always wished to visit Marrakech and this would be a fabulous opportunity, but she had no one to go with her for the week. Knowing I had a holiday imminent with a free week she telephoned me in great excitement asking if I would be 'up for it' and accompany her!

At that point, Ian had a fortnight's holiday due and so did I, but as frequently happened they overlapped and we only got one week at the same time. Mine was the first week, both of us for the second week and Ian the third week when I had to return to work. We had been making arrangements for our week together to spend time with relatives in the south of England and planned to visit Jane Austen's house. We also hoped to revisit one of our favourite places – the Isle of Wight.

My first week was free so I told Beryl I would go with her. As our holidays clashed, Ian's plans were that upon our return from the south coast, when I returned to work, he would do some walking and mountain climbing in the Lake District. These plans seemed excellent and I told Beryl I was happy to visit Morocco with her.

We were due to fly out on Sunday the fourteenth of March on an overnight flight, arriving in Agadir early on the fifteenth. On the Friday evening before leaving, Ian and I visited Helen and baby Jessica and confirmed everything was well organised and in place for my return. Both Ian and I were looking forward to our joint and individual trips. Of course Ian was leaving for his night-shift at that point, so as I was sitting on Helen's landing floor trying to set up my mobile phone for 'roaming' he stood at the top of the stairs wishing me a lovely trip and saying he would look forward to hearing about it. He patted me on the head and blew a kiss – very unusual actually, as he was never so demonstrative! He looked so smart, and always very young for his age, as he always had. I will never forget how well and handsome he looked that evening!

With a birthday on Christmas Eve he had just turned sixty-four three months previously. He also very much enjoyed his job; he had his own office which was a solitary situation dear to his heart, but during his breaks he would go up to the cafeteria and play a round of pool or snooker with his chums in the post office. He had made quite a lot of plans for his forthcoming retirement in nine months' time so the future looked bright. He said goodnight to Helen and I, and drove off to work.

Beryl and I flew out to Morocco in the early hours of Sunday morning, and upon arrival at the beautiful hotel in Agadir early next day we were amazed at the intricacy and beauty of the tiled floors (inside and out), the stunning view from our balcony across to the sea, and the fabulous tropical gardens below our windows. Of course Monday afternoon was spent at the 'Welcome Party' when we booked some trips for the week and then we were taken on a local tour visiting the hilltops, the site of the previous earthquake and then a walk around the harbour where the fishermen were hauling in millions of fish. We also made the acquaintance of a couple of camels with brave tourists having a ride on them!

The following day, Tuesday, we experienced a lovely Catamaran trip which included a nice meal and sat back enjoying the tranquillity of the hot sun and sea, the latter of which was just like a millpond. Beryl, being a true child of the sun, was sunbathing, whereas I tried to escape the heat, which was scorching. In fact as I was wearing a short-sleeved top I bore the line the sun burnt on my arms for almost a year, the heat was so intense! Beryl remarked on the glass-like surface of the sea, and I replied that it was like the 'calm before the storm'. Talk about prophecy!

Next day was our four-hour trip to Marrakesh, and Beryl was so thrilled. We were up at 5 a.m. as the dining room was opened especially for us to have an early breakfast, and we were on the coach by 6 a.m. I had been unable to get a mobile signal in Agadir, but an hour or so into the coach ride – Beryl being fast asleep at the side of me – my phone began to ring with a voicemail as it picked up a signal. It was very noisy on the coach with the rattle of the vehicle, the high-pitched voice of the Moroccan courier, and impossible for me to hear what the message was saying. All I could make out was a broken voice saying 'Mrs Glover, Accident and Emergency …' and then some disjointed numbers. It was another hour before we stopped for a coffee break and I had spent the time just wondering what on earth had happened back at home. For some reason I thought it must be one of my grandchildren, although common-sense should have told me that one of the girls would have phoned had that been the case.

So during our comfort stop I found a quiet place to listen properly but still could not make sense of the message. I quickly wrote down the numbers I could hear and then rang Helen as I knew she would be up early with Jessica, who was now two years old. Helen had no knowledge of anything being wrong with anyone, but took down the information I gave her and promised she would phone me back as soon as she discovered what was going on. I had to be content with that as it was time to re-join the coach and head for Marrakesh.

Helen rang back just as we arrived in the city. She was very reassuring, but told me it was Ian who had been taken ill at work in the early hours of the morning and was in hospital. He had suffered a stroke, but Helen told me he was receiving wonderful care and her husband took the day off work to look after the baby so he could take Helen and Margaret down to the hospital to be with their dad. I had to be content with that and just await further telephone calls.

I simply walked around in a fog following the group; similar to how it had been when the bad news about Jamie had been received. I was on automatic pilot, not knowing the severity of the stroke or what his prospects would be now. I just wanted to get the nearest and fastest aircraft home, but of course that was impossible. Nor could I request the coach driver to return to Agadir, as there were over fifty tourists in our group, so I trailed around after them all day, just longing for another call from Helen.

Unfortunately, that day involved many things such as visits to a perfume factory, carpet factory, the Berber market and a walk around historical places, finishing off in the evening with a meal and dancing entertainment. We were not due to leave Marrakesh until 10 p.m., meaning it would be 2 a.m. before we even got back to our hotel in Agadir. Being in such a large group of tourists I could not even stop at a public phone as I was terrified of losing the group in such an eclectic and rather scary environment. I can't say I really liked Marrakesh at all. The bazaar in particular worried me as it would have been easy to lose Beryl in amongst the many avenues and crowded stalls, and being bombarded by beggars and men with snakes wanting us to take photos with them (paying for the privilege) made me very panicky. I know they were only earning their living but in my current situation it was a nightmare.

Helen phoned me back in the late afternoon saying her dad had responded and knew his daughters were with him, but of course with being in the hospital environment I could not call them back as their phones would be switched off. It was a matter of just grinning and bearing it for the remainder of the day.

We were taken to some beautiful gardens in the centre of Marrakesh in the late afternoon called the Jardin Majorelle, where it was cool and shady, and, above all, peaceful. Beryl and I sat by a lovely pool and I calmed down a bit. My mind was a blank page really but obviously I needed to go home immediately, which could not be organised without the help of our courier at the hotel. He was not available until 9 a.m. the following morning.

By late afternoon before going for the meal (which I didn't want!) Beryl and I sat in a café drinking orange juice and Helen rang me back to tell me Ian was comfortable and she gave me the direct phone number so I could ring Manchester Royal Hospital when I returned to the hotel, and said they would tell me the situation.

At last we arrived back at the hotel around 2 a.m. Of course, I rang the hospital immediately from my bedside telephone, but the sister who had obviously only just come on duty was rather snappy and simply enquired, 'Well, aren't you coming to see your husband?' I explained where I was, in Morocco, but I don't think she believed me. I asked if I should come home immediately. 'Well if it was my husband I would,' she retorted, which wasn't helpful at all and actually rather sarcastic. That didn't help either.

Neither Beryl nor I slept that night, but at 9 a.m. after explaining the situation, our courier was wonderful. He took us to a travel agency in Agadir, and as the staff only spoke French or Moroccan he explained to them what we needed and we were there all day until 6 p.m. whilst they tried hard to find a flight back for us. There were no direct flights until the following Monday – which would of course have been the day we flew home anyway. I could not wait that long. I felt so sorry for Beryl as this had ruined her trip, but she was wonderfully supportive and enjoyed her time sitting by the pool until we managed to get a flight the following Friday. Neither of us wanted to do anything else.

Our courier collected us on Friday morning in his own car before he started work, and took us to the airport where he sorted out our flights and arranged for our luggage to be sent through direct to Heathrow. As there were no direct flights for another three days we had to make do with flying from Agadir to Casablanca, then Casablanca to Heathrow and Heathrow to Manchester. Our courier could not have been kinder or more helpful. Of course Helen had kept in touch over the past couple of days, but she had not told me everything, as I discovered later. For the moment I was just desperate to get back and those three days waiting for the flights were the longest I have ever experienced.

We did well until we landed at Heathrow only to find our connecting flight at 7 p.m. had been cancelled and the next available shuttle up to Manchester was the following day – Saturday – at 10 a.m. At that point I completely 'lost it' and said I would walk it if I had to! Beryl explained to the airport staff what was happening, and once again we found how helpful and wonderful flight attendants could be. They got us on a business flight an hour or so later, and although we did not have seats together it didn't matter – at least we were on the way back. We landed back home at 11 p.m. on the Friday night, British time. I had left my car in the Manchester Airport car park, so a special shuttle bus had been arranged to meet us and my car was there with the engine ticking over ready for us to depart. They even offered to drive me back home, had I wished it. People were so kind everywhere along the line, and it really renewed our faith in human nature.

Helen had not divulged to me the fact that Ian had suffered a further stroke on the day it first happened, and had since been in a coma. She warned me about all the machinery he was linked up to, but he had not responded again since his first day. When I walked into his hospital room I tried to be as normal as possible and just said, 'I don't know, Ian, I can't leave you for a moment, can I?' Helen had been telling him all day that I was on my way home, hoping he could hear her, and we all felt he had waited for me as his response was a huge grunt! That unexpected response made me feel reassured he had heard me, and had waited for my return.

Sadly, Ian died just twenty-four hours later on Sunday morning, the 21st of March, never having regained consciousness. There had been no sign at all that this terrible event was imminent, for if he had felt unwell or suspected anything was wrong he had not said so – but that was Ian. He kept a lot to himself. All we could think was that his asthmatic condition had deteriorated and his long-term use of steroids could have been contributory. His consultant confirmed this, and told us that sometimes allowing people to live a normal life with a chronic condition was the best, but that sometimes side-effects could cause damage.

We all lost the most wonderful person that day – a companion, father, husband and my best friend of thirty-six years. The girls and I felt that perhaps we should have noticed something was wrong somewhere along the line, and couldn't stop wondering if any of us in any way could have prevented what had happened. However, we had no choice but to pick up the pieces and carry on. The loss of their father knocked both of the girls sideways. They had always been so close to him, but they have ever since kept his memory alive for their children in photographs, albums and stories of his funny little ways and videos of him at home and on our holidays. This meant that little Charlie – Margaret's fifth child who was born four years later – could actually see his grandad. Not the same as knowing him, but he could hear him speak and see what a lovely man he was.

It had always been our habit to make a special meal for Ian on Christmas Eve so his birthday did not go unrecognised, and to this day Margaret still does 'Dad's meal' and sits round with whoever is available in the family. We all talk about him at those special meals and remember his funny little ways and how much we still love him.

I could no longer cope with the model train layout we had so painstakingly established together. I tried taking it apart and putting it back together a different way but it was no use. It meant nothing without Ian so I gave the rolling stock to my boss, who had his own layout in his loft, and dismantled the rest of it.

It was a rather weird year afterwards. So many people were devastated by Ian's loss, and despite his quiet, private ways it was amazing what great respect and fondness he had inspired in so many people with his gentle nature. When people came round to visit us after the funeral I was genuinely surprised at how many people he had worked with who had such deference and friendship with Ian, but they in turn had known nothing about him or even the fact that he had a family! It was lovely to know he had influenced and made such a mark on his colleagues with his gentle personality.

It is said that work is a panacea, so in between returning to work and sorting out all the millions of necessities after a bereavement, the time began to pass. My daughters, despite their own grief, had really looked after me following our loss – Helen had invited me to her home, let me rest on her settee day after day in the foggy mental state I was in, and made sure I was eating. She was so selfless and caring and knew, of course, that baby Jessica would play a huge part in cheering me up! And to do all this when she was deeply grieving herself of course.

Margaret was clinging to the few articles she had which belonged to her Dad and sought comfort in having them near to her. She had a hectic life with four children at that time, but thankfully had got remarried to a very kind and supportive husband. I was so proud of both girls: Helen for her wisdom, hiding her own emotion as best she could in order to care for me, and Margaret for treasuring her Dad's belongings and keeping him alive in my grandchildren's lives.

My colleagues at work were very understanding about the good and bad days. In a way, being completely alone again was not an unusual situation to me, as from the first year we had married Ian had done permanent night-shifts, so I was used to sorting things out, running a household, bringing the children up seven days a week and keeping myself occupied with various interests. Still, it was a huge void which had opened.

My wonderful friend, Sylvia, unknown to me, booked a week's holiday in Lloret de Mar in the May, and told me to pack as I was going away with her! This certainly assisted with the healing process. We had a very pleasant, quiet time and of course I knew life had to move forward.

I would never have had confidence to travel abroad alone but was restless and disconsolate at home. I knew it was therapeutic to get away a little and find new company, so I then decided to try a 'Just You' holiday to Lake Garda and made the snap decision to just 'do it'. This was only a few months after losing Ian but I knew that I really had to start being independent and would feel safe with a group of people. These holidays are not 'dating' holidays but simply for people of a similar age, being alone, who did not like travelling on their own – especially abroad. Single rooms were guaranteed and the privacy was there for solitude. It was perfect, for there was company if needed and it was also possible to go for a walk alone and have private memories and thoughts if required, but still feeling safe and well looked after in the hotel. I thought these holidays were perfect for me.

Next there was a holiday to Andalucía available which I liked the look of, and which included a visit to Gibraltar – somewhere Ian and I had wished to visit but had not had the opportunity. When I made enquiries, there was just one place on that trip left – should I take it, or not? In the end I plumped for it without giving it much thought, really, and after replacing the phone after booking it I was unsure whether it had been the right thing to do or not. Still, things didn't seem to matter too much at all in those months and it would be another break. The decision was made.

I looked up at the ceiling and said to Ian, 'We're going to Gibraltar at last.'

Little did I know what lay ahead, or that the old wooden spoon was stirring again. I didn't even consider what the outcome could be, but this was the very first step on a long and winding path, nurtured by fate perhaps, which would in due time – another ten years or so later – lead not only to a new life but to unimaginable discoveries of my own 'lost family' ...

Dad's Girls. George Ian Glover, 24th December, 1939 to 21st March, 2004

CHAPTER 13

Travelling Alone

———

I sat at my computer, pondering what the future might hold. Everything had changed. If only I could have offloaded the myriad things going around in my mind – what had happened, what was happening at present, and what would lie ahead. Of course, no one ever knows that. It seemed a little like a howling wilderness at this point, for Ian had gone so quickly and far, far, too soon. If only I could have defragmented my brain like a computer at that time I would gladly have done so.

Naturally work took up a lot of time, which kept my mind occupied and focused, so now there was also a holiday to Andalucía to look forward to. The journey began at Manchester Airport just later in the year after Ian had gone from us. He should have been there with me, looking forward to visiting the Rock together. Things felt very raw, but I hoped so much that this trip would bring new experiences and friends. It was going to do more than that, if only I had known. The old wooden spoon was *not* stirring up trouble for once, but was about to cook up the extremely unexpected!

On arrival in Andalucía I immediately teamed up with two lovely ladies in my group called Elspeth and Brenda, from Edinburgh and York respectively. For the entire holiday we went everywhere together and earned the nickname of 'The Three Musketeers'. Brenda was the eldest of us, an extremely intelligent lady, and Elspeth was a gifted artist who began to paint some wonderful scenery on the holiday. There were around thirty-two people in our group: six men and the remainder were ladies, as was usual our courier told us!

Our hotel in Mijas was beautiful – a breath of fresh air. The swimming pool outside was surrounded by fountains and gardens and we had some very interesting trips to look forward to. Gibraltar was the last on the list, to be taken on the penultimate day before we left for home. Guengirola, Mijas, Ronda, Grenada and the magnificent Alhambra Palace were on the itinerary, finishing up with Lake Chorro in the Guadalhorce Valley.

Most of my companions in the group chatted with one another as the week progressed, with 'good morning' greetings or exchanging a few words whilst queuing in the breakfast or evening meal ranks. In the evenings the six gentlemen stuck together (as they did all the time) and usually walked down the hill to the local public house where there was the customary football or sport on the widescreen television, whilst the ladies sat around the pool or in the lounge chatting.

I frequently still felt the need to be alone at that time, and sometimes just strolled round the gardens in the lovely evening air, admiring the flowers and views over the sea. There was always an underlying panic in me that once again, whilst holidaying abroad, something bad or serious would happen at home. On those occasions I would return to the group of ladies and join in their conversations to try and take my mind off those thoughts. Like me, many of the ladies had lost their husbands and we felt the comfort of 'being in the same boat', but no one was ever miserable or morose. We couldn't be, in such a beautiful place and warm sunshine.

On our visit to the Alhambra Palace, which was on the fourth day of our holiday, one of the gentlemen began talking to me about the history. This has always been one of my favourite subjects, and it wasn't long before we got onto the Tudors and walked a little way together during this discussion, but otherwise there was no exchange between us apart from

Gerald and I at the top of the Eiffel Tower.

the usual complimentary pleasantries. That was, however, until the day of the Gibraltar trip.

I had rushed downstairs for breakfast that morning, eager to share my enthusiasm for the trip with Brenda and Elspeth, as we had been fairly inseparable until that time. However when I sat down and began to talk about the day's plans, Brenda imparted the information that they were not actually going on the trip as both had visited Gibraltar before, so they intended to take the local train and have a shopping day instead. I was a bit nonplussed as, although I knew this was an 'extra-curricula' trip not included in the holiday as a matter of course, for some reason I had anticipated that most of our group would be participating. As it turned out, only seventeen of the group boarded the coach.

That was fine – we arrived in Gibraltar and were given a short coach trip around various viewpoints where we took photographs etc. We then boarded a minibus which took us further up the island to view the famous baboons and St Michael's Caves. One funny incident I will never forget was as

I came out of the caves and walked into a gift shop opposite: a large male baboon ran in, grabbed a Crunchie bar off the counter and ran out again. We were all laughing when the lady behind the counter told us, 'He's always doing that – Crunchies are his favourite!'

After our minibus tour we were given two and a half hours' free time and alighted in the main square where our courier advised us we could do as we wished. Out of the seventeen of us, fifteen headed straight for the duty-free shops. This was disappointing, as shops were the last thing on my mind, and I had envisaged quite a few of us would go the top of the Rock. I love to visit a place and look around so it was then I felt very nervous, as I had wished to catch the cable car to the top of the Rock but was extremely insecure at the prospect of perhaps missing the return coach if something happened to me whilst on my own. I had just seen the steep vertical cable cars, which were enough to instil horror in anyone. I asked our courier if I would be all right 'going it alone' up there, and of course she said there was no problem and pointed me in the direction of the cable car station.

At this point a soft voice from behind me suddenly said, 'I have no wish to go to the shops either, so would you mind if we went up in the cable cars together?' This was the tall pleasant gentleman I had spoken to in the Alhambra Palace, and of course was only too glad at the prospect of his company as I felt that at least if we *did* get stuck or left behind, at least there would be someone with me out of my own party!

We therefore precariously and somewhat nervously took the cable car ride to the top of the Rock of Gibraltar, which was absolutely amazing. During the assent the gentleman introduced himself as Gerald Marshall, and it turned out, strangely enough, that he lived in Wolverhampton – the place of my birth! Wow, what a coincidence. Could I learn anything about the place during our conversations? Although ascending a steep rock didn't really seem the right time to ask questions.

Once we reached the top station we were handed audio sets so conversation was greatly diminished and we each went our own way promising to meet for the descent when the tour was over. Just before we caught the cable car to make our way down once more, a little Japanese man approached Gerald and requested if he would be kind enough to take a photograph of his wife and himself, which Gerald did of course. He then gesticulated for Gerald to let him take a photo of 'us' together – how ludicrous, as of course we were total strangers! I was definitely 'wired for sound' as I had not only the audio set around my neck, but also my camcorder and camera. So, there we were – windblown, didn't even know each other and were completely overwhelmed with wires and cameras around our necks having our photographs taken at the top of the Rock of Gibraltar! Definitely not a dignified situation. Gosh, how we laughed! Looking back it is really strange to think how prophetic that photograph was!

Returning to Mijas on the coach we sat together, and Gerald told me he had chosen the holiday as it was the second anniversary of his wife's death, and he had not wanted to stay at home. The previous year he had found the memorial events too difficult to cope with and did not wish to go through that again. He preferred to be alone and spent the anniversary date in solitude the day we visited Ronda, alone with his own thoughts and memories, coping in his own way, which he told me had been very therapeutic.

Gerald had been born in Wales, but lived in Wolverhampton from the age of eleven, and had two daughters very nearly the same ages as my girls. He was quite amazed at the coincidence of my being born in the 'Black Country' as I told him I lived in Manchester, and we realised what a small world this can be.

The next time I saw Gerald was at our farewell meeting when we were all due to fly home the following morning. He came over to me and asked if I had an email address as he would like to send some of his photographs of Gibraltar to me when he got home. I thought it was safe enough to give him the email address in this way, but didn't think much more about it as he was flying back to Bristol and I was returning to Manchester.

People frequently promise such things at the end of holidays, but never follow through with them. However, two days later some lovely pictures arrived on my computer, including the one the Japanese gentleman had taken of us at the top of the Rock. What a vision! I looked like I had been dragged through a hedge backwards, and Gerald's t-shirt was not particularly brilliant! Of course I sent a 'thank you' email back to Gerald and this began a sort of correspondence between us. We certainly seemed to have a lot to talk about, and a few weeks later he asked if I would be willing to speak to him on the phone as we were enjoying our discussions about history, travel and music, books, musicals and all sorts of other interesting things. I was a fast typist and didn't find sending long emails in conversation a problem, but apparently it took him ages to do two lines! And so we started talking on the phone.

I had told Gerald of course, about losing Ian, and did not feel at all pressured by him as he, too, was still grieving for his wife. I had asked him about Wolverhampton and he told me a little bit about it, but had no idea where 89 North Road had been. In more recent years a huge ring road had been built around the city and he said parts of North Road and North Street had been demolished when this had been put in place. He thought it had been in the area where the famous Molineux Stadium was built, where Wolverhampton Wanderers played. Gerald was a huge Wolves supporter. My story fascinated him, but even though he attempted to discover some local information for me he only drew a blank.

At the beginning of November, Gerald asked me if I would like to meet up with him somewhere for the day, and suggested somewhere suitable around halfway between us would be best. Certainly I really enjoyed our conversations and thought he seemed very nice, but losing Ian was still very fresh in my mind and it felt rather disrespectful to think about spending a day with someone else – particularly a man. Also, I had no idea what Gerald was really like, as he was literally a stranger to me. I knew that meeting someone on a holiday can give a completely wrong impression of the person, so this suggestion of a day out with him was rather a concern to me. I was also very apprehensive about driving down to Wolverhampton from Manchester – going up and down the M6 with Ian and the girls on holiday trips was a lot different from taking a trip down there alone to meet someone who was really unknown to me!

I asked both my daughters what they thought. Margaret immediately said 'You go, Mum – you never know, he could be the love of your life.' I was a little shocked at this as I was not considering anything of the sort, but Helen more or less had the same outlook. 'You go, Mum, I'll call you on your mobile around one o'clock and if you are uncomfortable or want to get away you can just say your daughter needs you and make an exit.' So, that is what *they* thought! One or two of my friends said the same thing: 'It's only a day trip, go and have a nice time.'

Thinking about my life up to that point I had never, ever, taken a chance on anything. Mum and Gran would have been most negative and disgusted about this particular situation and considered I was being 'forward' and putting myself in danger. They would have scared me to death, but actually they were not there anymore and I was not contemplating any other relationship with Gerald than friendship. We seemed to get on so well, and as a cultured and intelligent man it was refreshing holding conversations with him. Somehow, I felt he was completely trustworthy, but I was notorious for being 'gullible'. Not the best reader of character, as I have always had a tendency to see only the best in people. No one now pushed me down with their prophetic doom of disaster or disapproval, and without Ian I had to seriously think for myself. Perhaps it was time to do so; I was in any event fifty-seven years old, not exactly young.

So, I decided to jump in feet first, probably for the first time in my life. We decided to meet up at Chatsworth House, which was roughly between where I lived near Manchester and around the same distance from Wolverhampton. Neither did it involve any motorways because I was very familiar with the route to Buxton and Chatsworth itself, where as a family we had visited many times when our daughters were growing up. In fact, Ian and I had spent a day there three weeks before we were married. Still, on the journey that day to meet Gerald I had a lot of misgivings – what on earth was I doing? Talk about being out of my 'comfort zone'. A couple of times as I neared the destination I almost backed out and returned home.

I arrived first and walked around the car park waiting for his car to arrive. About twenty minutes later he drove in and a hand came waving out of the driver's window as he drew up. I walked over to meet him and he was all smiles, just as he had been in Spain. There was no communication problem whatsoever; we just immediately started to talk, had a tour of Chatsworth House discussing everything in there and literally never stopped talking all day. We enjoyed a lovely meal in the restaurant and then strolled around the grounds along the side of the fabulous waterfall and the perimeter of the huge lake in front of the house itself, where high fountains were playing. It was quite a gloomy day all told and a bit muddy on the paths, but I don't think either of us gave it a thought. It was as if we had known each other for years and turned out to be one of the happiest and most wonderful days I had ever known. At the end of the afternoon we drove our cars into Buxton where we had some refreshment before parting to each drive home in different directions, but I think we both knew already that day was the beginning of something very special indeed.

Not long after our meeting at Chatsworth, Gerald invited me to visit him for the day at home in Wolverhampton. I accepted his invitation, although I was still concerned about the M6, but he promised to meet me in a layby just off the sliproad at the junction where I exited the motorway so I could follow him to his house. Once again we had a lovely day. He took me for a meal and we walked around Bridgnorth. This was a beautiful old town I was already familiar with, as the Severn Valley Railway was somewhere Ian and I had visited on several occasions considering Ian's love of steam trains, so I almost felt I was on home ground. We walked along the cliff top paths and Gerald told me some of the history of the old castle there, making me laugh by pretending to prop the leaning walls up at the place where they looked as if they would tumble down at any moment. He always made me laugh. It was such an innocent friendship at that time, without any pressure whatsoever but simply the enjoyment of each other's company: probably something which helped both of us to move on in our lives in a positive fashion. We were good for each other.

Visiting Wolverhampton that first time was quite spooky for me. I had been born there but obviously was taken away from the area at around two months old, after my registration. It would appear I had probably been born in the area where New Cross Hospital is situated, and I really felt quite jittery to be somewhere – for the first time in my life – where my life had actually begun. On later visits Gerald did take me through the grounds of the hospital and showed me the old red brick buildings which still remained after the workhouse was taken over by the NHS in 1948, and I was probably born in one of those. Many buildings had been demolished. This was a difficult place for my friend to go as he had very sad memories of the years his wife had been so ill there. The hospital, however, is nowhere near the location of where North Road had been, so that remained a question to be answered. I still felt number 89 may have been the home of a relative of my birth family where Vera had been staying at the time I was born.

I did not see Gerald again after my first visit to Wolverhampton through Christmas and New Year until February the following year, when he took me to London for my birthday to see *The Woman in White* which was a new Andrew Lloyd Webber musical.

On further visits to Wolverhampton he showed me where North Road had been, but it was impossible to discover the location of number 89 as only a small piece of the road still existed. The old properties which would have lined North Road had been demolished in the 1960s to make way for halls of residence for Wolverhampton University.

Gerald was not unlike Ian in many ways. They had the same 'gentle man' air about them, but whereas Ian was not a conversationalist, Gerald adored being with and chatting to people and he loved to take funny photographs, such as posing on motorbikes or standing with the wax people in various funny attitudes in Madame Tussauds on visits to London – making other people laugh as well as myself with the funny faces he would pull. He was a tall slim man, being 6 foot 2 inches and quite an imposing figure, always smart and well dressed. Golf was his main hobby, which he played very regularly as he had taken early retirement after the death of his wife and he was the club's treasurer for some years.

And so over the next four years, gradually, our relationship developed and our worlds became completely merged. My two daughters loved Gerald and almost looked on him as a second father as time went on. There was objection to his wish to remarry, but that was not our intention for some time. We shared so much and Gerald was with me in Manchester on the very day my youngest grandson, Charlie, was born. We treated each other's homes very much as our own, helping with gardening etc. and has such fun making our plans.

We shared a lot of similar ideas about many things, as well as interests, driving, sense of humour, music and theatre. The main difference between Ian and Gerald was that Ian very much enjoyed his own company whereas Gerald was a really "sociable" person – he loved being amongst friends for meals and thoroughly enjoyed any celebrations. However, personality-wise they would have got on well together had they ever been able to meet!

And so for four joyful, wonderful years, Gerald and I shared such happiness. One or other of us would drive up (or down) the M6 every weekend, for although Gerald was already retired I was still working full time. I would drive down to Wolverhampton straight after work on a Friday evening when he would have a lovely meal waiting for me, or he would drive up to Manchester on a Friday afternoon ready to meet me after work. We visited all sorts of places together – daytrips and weekends in England, holidays in Scotland, Sicily, Minorca, Madeira and a magical three day break in Paris, which I shall never forget. Gerald's friends became mine and vice versa, he asked me to assist him with his treasurer's duties at his local golf club where he played three or four times a week, and as our lives became completely inseparable it became more and more difficult to be apart. Neither of us could ever believe we had found such happiness once again and we began to make tentative plans.

As I approached my sixtieth birthday and was due to retire we began more seriously to discuss our future, which we wanted to share together. It took a lot of discussion and planning. We had three options – for him to move to Manchester, myself to move to Wolverhampton or for us both to sell our homes and purchase a joint one somewhere in between. The latter was not sensible as we would be moving to an unknown area and would not have known anyone. Taking into account Gerald's social life and responsibilities at the golf club, and the fact he was an avid Wolverhampton Wanderers supporter, it didn't take long to decide I would make the move. My daughters had no problem with this as they could see how happy we were. We were about to live our dream.

CHAPTER 14

Living the Dream

───

Big plans had been the order of the day now for the past two years prior to my retirement. So, on my actual sixtieth birthday, after leaving my office farewell party with my new car (complete with its ' Cherish' number plate Gerald had given me for my special birthday), full to the brim with 'last' items I wished to take with me, I made the southward journey to my new home with Gerald.

We had discussed everything that needed to be sorted out at this point, and upon my arrival in Wolverhampton Gerald placed a beautiful diamond ring on my finger. However we had decided to wait for a full year before marrying, in order to be certain we could settle down as a couple, and if that had not turned out well I would be able to purchase my own property from the proceeds of the sale of my house and we could still spend time together but live apart. In later life it is not always easy for two people to commence a life together when they are 'set in their ways'. However, life for us together was simply magical – everything seemed to be so simple, so right, and so happy.

Of course, we talked about our respective spouses a lot and treasured their memories. My daughters were now eighty-three miles away but plenty of visits were planned and the future looked rosy. Because of this distance it would have been very difficult to sell both houses at once, so I had made the huge decision to sell mine first and move down to Gerald's home. He had a detached house, but as it was not particularly large none of my furniture would have fitted. I had therefore sold or given away everything I had apart from personal items, and simply took with me the things I treasured most. The most difficult thing for me was parting with Mum's piano. It had been her twenty-first birthday present from her parents, and of course I had learnt to play on it as a child. Thankfully, one of the ladies I worked with knew a family with two little girls who were learning, so I was glad to see it go to a new home where it would be well looked after.

We intended our first year together to be one of planning and making changes. Gerald decided that if we settled down well he would put his house on the market later that year and, when it was sold, we would pool our resources and buy a bungalow between us. Our new home would be completely redecorated and brand-new furniture purchased which we both liked. Although nothing was chosen at that time because it was too soon, we actually saw three or four properties we liked, and it was very exciting to have plans.

I had kept my possessions to a minimum and big discussions took place between us as to how we would fulfil matters legally, in terms of being fair to our four daughters when we bought a home together. I knew the pros and cons of how to do this and explained it all to Gerald so he was perfectly happy. My daughters were really pleased for us, but I never really felt Gerald's were, although they knew nothing of our personal plans in which *everyone* was catered for. There is a big difference between purchasing a property as 'tenants in common' and as 'joint tenants', which would have been inappropriate.

So, for the initial six weeks I started to put some little roots down and we really lived our dream. We were so happy. I began training to be a guide at nearby Wightwick Manor, which is a National Trust property, and Gerald continued with his beloved golf. I loved living in Wolverhampton, which is much the same as any other city, but of course I had a personal connection knowing it was the place of my birth, and I intended to discover as much as I could about those beginnings in due course. The worst thing to come to terms with was the notorious ring road – not a fabulous experience!

It was wonderful now to experience the proximity to places such as Hereford, Worcester, Ludlow, the Cotswolds and Shrewsbury, which were only an hour or so away by car, plus many wonderful National Trust properties, Ironbridge Gorge and such beautiful rural countryside which for me in the past had only been known as holiday destinations. And here a lot of them were – right on the doorstep! Of course I realised why the West Midlands bore the label of the 'Black Country' with its wonderful industrial past, but now there was nothing 'black' about it and I loved exploring new places where Gerald took me and started to become very happy in my new area.

Those first few short weeks were everything we had hoped for with plans for holidays, a new home and routine. We had sorted everything out to our mutual satisfaction and life was taking on a real shine. We set up a monthly household budget so I could pay my half of the monthly outgoings into Gerald's account at this time as I still wished to be considered

Ironbridge, where Gerald was a guide.

independent and did not in any way wish to appear I was taking advantage. Unfortunately, so far there had been little time for us to put anything in place regarding our relationship or future plans, but I had made the huge move with my eyes wide open and forty years of legal experience in which I had seen what can (and often does) happen. In my case I felt reasonably secure with my finances locked in the bank for the first year, which was a cushion should anything go wrong. What a good job! We were living on a fluffy pink cloud of happiness, but disaster was on the way!

Early in April, Gerald started to feel quite dizzy and had dreadful exhaustion, which meant he couldn't do very much and had to stop driving. Visits to the doctor didn't really explain what was going on so there were good and bad days. Unfortunately it was a downward situation, so by June his doctor referred him to a neurologist at New Cross Hospital. The previous evening before his appointment Gerald had written a list of nineteen questions he wanted answers to: why was he so exhausted (he couldn't even walk from the bedroom to the bathroom by now without having to stop and rest)? Why was he so dizzy? And some other items of importance. I sat in the corner of the room whilst the specialist answered the questions, and after examining Gerald he pronounced it was labyrinthitis and post-viral fatigue. Gerald felt happier as we left the hospital at having some sort of diagnosis, for he felt he had an explanation and that it would improve over the next few weeks. It did not. It got worse. What a tragedy that consultant had not run an MRI scan, as disaster *may* have been avoided. It would have revealed he had already suffered three 'TIA' experiences.

After the hospital visit Gerald was much more cheerful, but he did not seem to rally or really get better. We had two short five-day holidays, firstly to Poole in Dorset and then to Lyme Regis, feeling sea-air might do him good. I had to do all the driving, which was not a problem, and during those two breaks he certainly felt refreshed, but there were odd days when he could do nothing at all or even get out of bed. When we returned home from Lyme Regis he certainly felt refreshed and steadier in himself and even drove round a few local roads to see how he went on. This pleased him so much as he felt he was now recovering and optimistically started saying we would book a 'proper' holiday soon.

Sadly this was not to be. On the 31st of August I awoke to the realisation my beloved Gerald had just suffered a huge stroke. He was propped up in bed staring icily ahead, and when I waved my hand in front of his face there was no response. Nothing. His beautiful blue eyes stared ahead unseeingly.

This was the worst nightmare come true. Responders had been immediate to my phone call and later I sat at the hospital on my own waiting to hear if Gerald had survived. His sister and her husband came a little while later and I will never forget her kindness. She came in and said, 'I'm here for my brother, Judith, but you need a sister.' How wonderful is that?

Everything which followed seemed to be a blank void where actions were taken automatically. In a matter of a few moments the cards were dealt and Gerald was locked in his body completely for the rest of his life. I do not intend to record how the next two years went by, but suffice to say he had lost everything a human being *could* lose. The remainder of his existence was just that – an existence. His mind was still there and he had survived initially, but it was no longer a 'life' for him. He could literally talk with his eyes once the first few weeks passed but could not read, write, walk, talk, was fed by tube and over the next two years became totally institutionalised. He was not allowed to return home after the first six weeks, although I have always felt his best chance of a decent recovery would have been made at home, but that decision was out of my hands. I had no say in the matter.

Sadly, Gerald never returned home. His time was between hospital, rehabilitation and then 'Sunrise Senior Living' for onward National Health treatment. Sadly this 'onward' care only lasted a further six weeks and thereafter, although I tried to help him with some sort of physiotherapy, it proved too much for me as he was heavy, and no outside influence was set up to help take over.

At this difficult time following Gerald's stroke I was in something of a 'zombie' state where everything seemed unreal. I soon came down to earth though in learning how things had changed dramatically and where I stood. Living in Gerald's home was a nightmare, although I spent between three and five hours with him – wherever he was at the time – on a daily basis. I never wanted to go back to his house as memories of that fateful morning met me at the front door every time, so I would stay out as late as possible and then immediately go up to bed to try and shut out the pain. I guess I still tried to be positive and hope some sort of improvement would happen – I dreaded losing him.

When it became certain he was definitely not going to return home due to the intense twenty-four care he now needed, I found myself between a rock and a hard place. Certain 'rules' were put in place which I was expected to adhere to, and on occasion I would return to the house to discover a keyholder had let themselves in without asking me or even telling me they were doing so. Generally the house was no longer my refuge once Gerald had been carried out of it. The worst thing was that all my personal belongings and private papers were there of course, and I had nowhere else to go. I felt completely unwelcome and almost like a displaced person. When I ventured to explain how difficult it felt to be alone in the house now, I was simply told, 'Well it isn't worse for anyone, is it?' Maybe that was true?

I had certainly been in a terrible state by witnessing what had happened to Gerald, but the incomprehensible way I was now treated meant I was doubly affected by what had happened and felt completely destroyed by the pit I had fallen into. Everything seemed black, with no future, no home of my own or, indeed, few possessions, no furniture, and not even the sanctity of returning to a place where I had been so happy, as it was no longer a place of refuge. I did not want Gerald's house or any part of it – it was not 'home' without him. He had been my home. I was financially independent and able to start a new life, but still I clung on to the rapidly fading hope that he would make some recovery and eventually regain some sort of life.

Always having had a distinctive way of showing his feelings facially, Gerald could still convey a lot by his expressions, and sadly I know he was aware of what had happened to him. I have never dared to try and imagine what he experienced when he recovered sufficiently to realise the condition he was in, but he fought like mad to make progress. His nurses knew how hard he tried to follow their instructions and could see what a lovely person he was, but sadly the odds were stacked against him recovering from the very beginning. Too much damage had been done. I have not, however, ever known just how much he knew about the undercurrents, and have always hoped and prayed that no pressure or unnecessary information was imparted to him. I guess the loss of his voice was probably the worst thing, as at least if he could have spoken for himself we would have known what he wanted and what we could have done for him properly.

Gerald had always sung along to one of his favourite songs by Neil Diamond – 'If There Were No Dreams'. I can always picture him singing it to me, and perhaps in some way prior to his illness there had been messages in that song. It was certainly very appropriate when I listened to it in later times.

And so for the six months following his stroke, I struggled to throw off the feeling of being more or less a homeless person. Everything had gone – all the hopes, dreams of our new life together and the loss of someone I loved so much. However, his friends, neighbours and closest childhood friends were absolutely wonderful and supportive, and certainly pulled me through those dark days. I felt sick every time I stepped into the hall when I returned to the house, as the unspeakably horrific memories of that first morning always crowded in when I opened the front door. My own daughters and friends, albeit up in Manchester, also gave me a lot of emotional support, and it was amazing how everyone rallied round and helped me the best they could. A few of my friends actually came down to spend a few days with me from time to time, as did Helen, and I did not ask permission as to whether they could stay or not as I was past caring. At least during the time Gerald was in Sunrise, visiting times were completely free and I could go whenever I wished and stay as long as I wanted to. By the second year they even gave me a meal if I was there at those times!

The following January when Gerald was well established in Sunrise for permanent care, one of his friends took me down to the Bistro for a coffee and told me I was 'going down the pan' and 'wouldn't be of any use to Gerald' if I continued the way I was going. He said, 'You know what you need to do – get your own place now, and if Gerald ever returns home you can go back to be with him.' I knew this was the right thing to do, and that little lecture pushed me to do exactly what he recommended.

It was difficult, but I really needed to leave his house where I had struggled to live now for over four months on my own, and start to build my own security again. Gerald's sister came with me to look at a few properties and I found the most perfect little one-bedroomed flat which had been fully refurbished just a year before. It had a brand-new roof, laminate floors throughout, a beautiful bathroom with bath and walk-in shower, a fully fitted kitchen, large lounge and bedroom. It was a first-floor property, and also had loft storage and a small garden outside, unusual for a flat. Another benefit was that it was fully furnished. Not with furniture I particularly would have chosen, but the sellers actually lived in

Spain and had just used the flat to stay in whilst visiting relatives in England, so it was complete in a Mediterranean style and an agreement was made for me to purchase the existing furniture. I could walk straight in and live there without lifting a finger to do anything whatsoever. This was heaven-sent as, of course, I had no furniture of my own at that time, and by the May I moved into my own flat. How wonderful it was to close the front door and build my own little sanctuary.

I had written a long letter to Gerald's family two weeks before moving explaining my reasons for doing this, but never received a reply. It seemed the correct and courteous thing to do and of course I realised what had happened to their father was dreadful for them, too. It is a pity we could not have supported each other. I had offered to revisit his house every couple of days to keep an eye on it and make sure everything was all right, but when I went to the house two days later all the locks had been changed . . .

Owing to Gerald's condition and his height, he was never able to sit in a normal wheelchair, and it was almost two years before his sister and I managed to arrange for a special customised chair to be made for him. This meant I could wheel him into the lift at Sunrise and take him down to the ground floor for short visits – he had by then been stuck in the same room for all that time as it had been impossible to get him out. The special chair was extremely heavy, but he appeared to be comfortable in it and the chair had special adaptations on the back to take his feeding tube. The chair could not be taken outside, but at least getting him out of that room was a big improvement and meant he could be taken into one of the lounges where there were other people and entertainment. He was not really able to enjoy very much but it is comforting to think that at least he had *some* change of scenery for a very short time. I had spent five or six hours virtually every day of the past two years with him trying to bring at least half an hour of sunshine and some sort of 'normality' back to him for a short time. These had been anguished, heart-breaking years in a terrible situation, which had been purgatory for him and those who loved him. In his last week my prayers had changed from, 'Please help him make some recovery', to 'Please just take him.' On that final day I had driven over to a local store and had seen the most beautiful rainbow. I had felt it was a sign – and it was! How I wish I had taken a photograph of that wonderful sight.

Gerald's battle to survive ceased on the 28th of March 2010 when I received a short message from one of his daughters to say 'Dad's gone'. That was it.

I did not attend Gerald's funeral, as I did not feel I could cope with it, but I did manage to spend time with him in the Chapel of Rest the day before, having had to get 'permission'! No one had been given details of the arrangements, and on the day of the funeral I was at home – my daughter had come to stay with me, as had my friend Lynne and another friend, so I was not alone. However, it seems that when the service was over no refreshments were available and people were left standing around not knowing where to go – particularly two couples who had driven up from the south of England very early that morning. So, to cut a long story short I finished up with twenty-six people in my flat and twelve of us decided to walk up to the local Merry Hill pub for a meal before everyone returned home.

The entire golf club where Gerald had played for many years had turned out in their beautiful green jackets and delayed a match until the afternoon in order to pay their respects to someone who was very much liked, and a few months later a memorial cherry tree was planted by the first tee, complete with a memorial plaque in Wolves colours commemorating Gerald. That was so nice.

The day after the funeral seemed strange. I had been retired for two and a half years, and yet had experienced no 'real' retirement apart from the six short weeks when Gerald and I had really lived our dream. Now the emptiness of the forthcoming years without Gerald and Ian stretched ahead, and my flat was not yet really a 'home'. It was my own space containing my belongings, but I still did not feel settled. I knew there was quite a process to go through before the pieces could be picked up once more, and in my heart I knew even then that no one could ever again take the place of the two wonderful men I had loved and lost. How privileged I had been to have them both in my life; they had been the best and truest of men, my best friends, companions and soulmates, albeit in quite different ways. I had been very blessed and realised even at that time I would never get over what I had witnessed Gerald having to bear. It left a permanent scar which would heal a little in time but never disappear.

So, as I opened the curtains that first morning I looked around at my new, shining, tidy flat, took a deep breath and stuck the wooden spoon out of sight as deep into the drawer as I could. I didn't want it stirring up any more difficulties in the foreseeable future, and it was time to wipe all the old memories out of the computer hard-drive and start to enter some new things, times, places and friends. This would take time, but time was all that was left to me now.

One huge decision was whether to stay in Wolverhampton or return to the Manchester area. Yes, it was time to take another fork in the road and discover what was around the bend. At least I was in the right place to make further enquiries about the start of my life – yes, that could be interesting, a tiny flicker of light told me.

Perhaps there *was* still a reason for my being here after all ...

CHAPTER 15

To Leave or Stay . . .

My laptop sat in front of me, but my mind was a complete blank. There were so many things to sort out, but nothing made sense. The hard-drive in my brain was playing over and over, days and nights seemed to merge into one and there was no routine any more. It had become second nature over the past two years to grab a quick snack around noon and then set off for Sunrise, so on many occasions now I found myself preparing things to take – and then realised it was no longer applicable. I would turn around, sit down again. What to do, where to go?

Apart from the normal grieving process I believe there was an element of delayed shock. The world seemed empty now and nothing mattered. I didn't have any work to go to – and yet that seemed like only yesterday, a mere six weeks ago from leaving the office to Gerald's imprisonment. What had happened in between belonged to some other planet. I had not really adjusted to retirement or started to look around and put other things in place to help pick up the pieces. Actually the three years following my loss were like a howling wilderness, as my thoughts were completely out of control or sense. Nature heals in her own time and cannot be hurried, but over a year needed to pass before I began to look around and try to be more sensible. Of course I was thankful Gerald was no longer suffering, but I was not needed any more.

One thing I did know is that I wished to stay where I was. There was no pressure put upon me to return to Manchester, and with my little flat so beautifully situated there was no point in leaving it. As already stated, although people had previous assumptions that the 'Black Country' was grim, I realised this was not the case at all. Improvements in working conditions, the loss of many factories and industries had lightened the area in many ways, and I was only minutes from the most beautiful unspoilt country and lovely little villages.

As the months went by and I felt claustrophobic staying indoors, I would drive twenty minutes down the road to Bridgnorth and walk around appreciating the history, lovely air and memories of visiting the Severn Valley Railway when Ian was alive. Being a tourist town it felt was as if I was on holiday, witnessing people enjoying their ice-creams, the steam trains, the beautiful River Severn and bustling shops. Within an hour I could go further afield once I plucked up courage on my own to visit many different places. It was a wonderful central area to live.

Shortly after moving into my flat I was attempting to make sense of my little garden plot when I heard a cheerful female voice wish me 'good morning'. As my flat was one of six, the voice came from the other end of the building, and I was about to encounter Maureen for the first time – a true Black Country girl! In the years that followed we became the closest pals and this was the start of a wonderful friendship. She, too, had experienced extreme personal problems and only recently moved into her flat. Over the next year or so we helped each other in many ways and built a lifetime support which continues today.

Through Maureen I met other ladies – Jenny was instrumental in introducing me to a craft class held weekly, where I soon made other friends, and a friend still living in the Manchester area advised me to join the U3A, where I could join groups and learn new things. The 'University of the Third Age' was something I had never heard of before, but it is for people in their 'third' age of life – e.g. retired – and this became an absolute lifeline for me. It was not easy at first to walk alone into a room full of strangers, but as the U3A groups are often held in peoples' homes it seemed a little easier. Initially I found the courage to attempt the local history group. After all, if I was staying in Wolverhampton I needed to learn about the local history and wondered if that activity might reveal more about the information I needed regarding myself?

The Creative Writing Group turned out to be my life-saver, as having 'homework' to do each month meant I had to sit down at the computer and turn on my vivid imagination once more to create 'new' things, rather than dwell on what had just happened. From early childhood I have loved writing poems and short stories, so now I could channel those pleasures into something positive.

It was not too long before I purchased a sat nav, and once more this was a golden opportunity. It gave me the confidence to drive much further distances, knowing I could always 'get home' if I got lost! I explored the highways and byways, down little country lanes bounded by high hedges just to see where they led, and started to familiarise myself with the area much better. This little machine also brought visits to many friends around the country, taking away the need for lengthy map reading. Sometimes it was difficult to go long distances as it would be easier to simply hide away at home, but with a bit of self-discipline it reaped rewards and made me stronger. However, it does take time to readjust and put down new roots. Interest was revived in old 'roots' of course, for at least I was now living in the best place to discover more!

Without a doubt it was not until three years had actually passed since leaving the Manchester area that life really began to pick up its pieces for me. The first two years had been bound up with Gerald and his needs, the third with slow recovery. Through the Local History Group I discovered that Wolverhampton Archives held excellent information, and made a point of visiting the beautiful building (the old

Molineaux Hotel where Gerald and Ann had celebrated their wedding celebrations in 1968). The people who worked at the Archives were lovely, and as I explained what my search was about – finding information about 89 North Road and 376 Wolverhampton Road – it soon became apparent they didn't have a clue what I was talking about! However, they did their best and dug out the Wolverhampton Red Book and were extremely interested in my story about being born in Wolverhampton. Obviously, I had explained what I was searching for, and promised faithfully that if I ever managed to find information I would put a booklet together and donate a copy of it to themselves and the local library. It was now mid-2012 and I was about to unwittingly embark on a search which was to take three years, and was genuinely the most therapeutic mission to ever happen for me.

Discovering 376 Wolverhampton Road was comparatively easy, as it had been the address of the old workhouse and is where modern-day New Cross Hospital had been built. So that was one discovery to start with!

So, where was 89 North Road, and was it a private residence or something else? The Archives kindly assisted me in tracing some very old maps of Wolverhampton dating back before the advent of the notorious ring road. The address was on my birth certificate as the place my birth mother had been living at the time of my birth, so I had assumed it was either the family home or that of a friend or relation. Wolverhampton Road appeared to be near the modern New Cross Hospital, so I wondered if that had been a maternity home or suchlike, and was on the certificate as where I was born. So, where were they originally?

Incredibly, two maps were produced to me – one showing North Road and the second one superimposing 1937-1938 on top of the older map. On the first map was an area showing a 'memorial home', and on the superimposed map it stated 'The Mrs Legge Memorial Home'. This was the first time I had come across the address being a home, as that was not written on any birth certificate, so my 'Life Jigsaw' was about to start being filled in! Wow.

I couldn't wait to discover just where the building had been. This was not easy, as North Road and North Street merged one into the other, but by minutely studying the maps I now took a walk on foot to discover just where my birth mother had stayed in Wolverhampton. The properties along North Road were demolished in the 1960s to make way for Wolverhampton University halls of residence, as already mentioned, but Hill Street, which originally ran down one side of the memorial home gardens, has completely disappeared. However, I got the general idea of the correct position and couldn't wait to find out about this home – what it was, what happened there, and to see if there were any pictures of it to be found.

This was a very difficult task, but the Wolverhampton Red Book in the Archives did furnish some interesting information. My journey of discovery had begun!

Firstly, I discovered that the Mrs Legge Memorial Home was officially dedicated and opened at 89 North Road, Wolverhampton on the 8th of February 1913 following the death, little more than a year before, of the Hon. Mrs Augustus Legge, who had been the wife of the bishop of Lichfield. Mrs Legge had done much charitable and church work amongst women and girls, and for the friendless and fallen, so therefore a large number of her friends decided to forward a movement, initiated by Mrs Legge shortly before her death, to provide a maternity home for young unmarried mothers. The Mrs Legge Home therefore resulted, providing a house capable of receiving, initially in its original state, six inmates in 1913.

The coverage of the opening in the Staffordshire Advertiser stated, 'The residence in North Road, Wolverhampton, which has been secured is a most suitable one in every way'. The

Committee obtained possession on New Year's Day 1913. I quote:

The house, which was formerly occupied by a Mr and Mrs Davis, is well screened from the road by trees and iron palisading, and the interior accommodation is well adapted for the purposes of a home. On the ground floor are located the Lady Superintendent's room, committee room and girls' workroom opening out onto a fairly large garden with good lawns, also kitchen and washhouse. On the upper floor, two large bedrooms have been cubicled off to form four smaller ones. There is also another small bedroom and a large room used as a sick bay. Accommodation is also provided for the Lady Superintendent upstairs. At the rear of the house a room, approached by a stairway, has been converted into a small Chapel.

The opening ceremony of the home on the 8th of February 1913 was largely attended, the weather fortunately being fine although rather dull. The invited guests assembled about 3 p.m. and after an inspection of the institution, which elicited unstinted approval of the executive committee's arrangements, the dedication service was proceeded with. The bishop of Stafford in his opening remarks expressed pleasure at the large attendance, which, he said, showed clearly that there was a great number who took a real interest in the object of the home and also in the reason for its initiation.

Speaking of the reality and the need for the work. Dr Were said they all knew how much the late Mrs Legge had it at heart, and how it was for this that she made her very last appeal. He proceeded to read a letter which the bishop of Lichfield had written to him, from which is extracted the following:

The Palace, Lichfield, 1 Feb. 1913. My dear Bishop – Let me ask you to tell all those dear friends who are present how deeply I feel their kindness. How earnestly I pray for the work with which they are associating themselves that it may be the means of saving many whose conditions and opportunities in life forbid us to condemn them harshly, but rather bid us, whose environment has always been so different and whose opportunities have been and are so many and so great in comparison of theirs, do what we can to pull them out of the mire, to save both them and their little ones from a life of misery and sin ... it was the deep sense that such work is the work of Jesus Christ that the meanest soul is dear to Him which led my dearest wife to give so much of her time and thought to the development in the diocese of every form of rescue and preventative work ...

In some ways I found this quite amusing, although I am sure the bishop was very genuine it did sound a bit like Mr Collins from *Pride and Prejudice*!

The Maternity and Child Welfare Committee were asked several times to pay for girls going into the Mrs Legge Memorial Home. A letter contained in the minutes dated 19 May 1925 from a Miss Wood of the Mrs Legge Memorial Home asks the council to agree to pay a lump sum, or to a payment of 15/0d per week for each girl and a 15/6d confinement fee, so by this time the fee had been raised from 12/6d which it was in 1922 to 15/0d. The committee accepted the latter, but insisted that this would only be with the approval of the Ministry of Health before admission, and on the understanding that the previous character, health etc. of the case was satisfactory and that the girl conformed to the rules of the institution.

On the 15th June 1920 a building notice was issued approving plans to extend the home, providing accommodation for seventeen girls from the previous six. The home was in use at North Road until 1960 and after moving to 134 Tettenhall Road it existed there until it, too, was demolished in 1975.

The advert in the Wolverhampton Red Book for 1922-1923 reads:

The Mrs Legge Memorial Home, 89 North Road. Affiliated to the Lichfield Diocesan Association Preventative and Rescue Work. The Home is intended for young unmarried mothers of *previously respectable character*. Every girl is expected to remain in the Home with her child for at least six months after its birth. Board of Guardians and friends are expected to guarantee payment of 12/6d per week for each case before admission. Girls are trained for domestic service and are taught the care of their children. Suitable employment is found for them in leaving, and foster parents for their infants.

I imagine 12/6d per week was a considerable amount of money for the girl's family to find, as there were no benefits in 1947.

Those involved in these homes believed that with a steady diet of religious and domestic training, motherly care and guidance, their charges could be saved and returned to the 'glory of their womanhood'! Domestic service was an important part of the redemptive work of these homes. Because many of the homes only took first-time offenders and girls from otherwise respectable backgrounds, they felt assured of their success. Interestingly, out of the seventeen girls from the Mrs Legge Memorial Home that were discharged in the years 1934-1935, six were sent into service, two were married and nine returned home.

Once I had started these investigations in 2012 it was difficult to know how to proceed to gain any further information about what had happened to me, so the best way forward seemed to be to insert a letter in local papers – *The Bugle* and *The Express* and *Star*. These newspapers both had a wide circulation throughout the Black Country. Would anyone have information or memories about the Mrs Legge Home? It was a long shot, and I had not really anticipated much reaction, but started to receive many letters and emails from different places within quite a large radius of Wolverhampton, and from these it became very apparent that through the years a lot of people have wished to know what and where 89 North Road was.

One lady sketched what she remembered and told me:

'I remember the home. We used to go to school down Hill Street and I used to look over a very high wall to the home from my auntie's back bedroom window. I remember the nappies blowing on the line and some young women in smocks – prams and small cots with babies sometimes crying. The nurses looked like nuns because of the headwear. I recall the nurses in the Co-op shop with navy-blue macs belted tightly and very stern. It was a lovely looking house lined with trees and bushes at the front. I remember the Chestnut tree in Hill Street, some branches going over the front garden with big pinky red flowers on. We did not ask questions in those days – as my aunt used to say 'ask no questions you will hear no lies'. The sign was navy or dark blue with gold letters'.

I received letters with personal memories relating to either themselves or their family, and these are some excerpts from various correspondence:

'I started work in 1945. I was fourteen at the time and the bus I travelled on into town went along North Street. I used to see girls outside this place, with babies in very big old-fashioned prams – I think the girls wore some sort of overall or apron, all dressed the same. It was not until I got older that I realised most of the babies would be adopted and that the girls had come from different towns and cities so that when they went home without their babies no one knew anything about the babies they had left behind.'

'My mother was pleased to see your letter, especially as it

said the establishment "for mothers of previously respectable character".'

'I was actually born at 89 North Road, Wolverhampton, July 1935 and then transferred to the workhouse in Stafford ... I never knew the home had a title and anything about it being for unmarried mothers. For years I wanted to trace it and always believed it was where my mother's family lived and actually went over to find it but it had been demolished. I was so disappointed'.

'The Mrs Legge Memorial Home goes back as far as the early part of the First World War. My father was born there in September 1917 and for many many years I tried to find the records. Unfortunately no one could (or would) help. I know these records would be very sensitive and private, so maybe there was good reason.'

'Eventually someone kind in the Lichfield Diocese sent me some info about the home. It was often shown on birth certificates as 89 North Road, Wolverhampton.'

'We have been researching our family history for ever! We were very interested as my elder stepsister was at one point

89 North Road, taken shortly before its demolition. This was the Mrs Legge Home.

living there ... The baby was born at New Cross Hospital in January 1947 but we could never make out why she was living at 89 North Road at the time'.

'My sister gave birth to a baby boy ... I went to see them; he was beautiful. My parents refused to have anything to do with him. They used to line up all the babies in Mrs Legge's Memorial Home in their prams outside in the freezing cold December weather. My sister had to wash his nappies by hand in cold water. She was only fifteen and the baby was sent for adoption by a family, but when my sister returned home she was met by her partner (the father of the baby) and they refused to sign the final adoption papers, so a few months later the baby was returned back to my sister and her partner. They married, had more children and are still very happy. My sister refuses to talk about what she went through at the time, but I can still remember what she went through at Mrs Legge's Memorial Home.'

I myself had one conversation with an eye witness who had lived opposite the Mrs Legge Home at North Road. As a child she was given a weekly piano lesson in the front room, and would see new parents arriving to take the babies. She told me it was very upsetting.

When I did meet my own birth mother, Vera, I asked her if she could remember where she had been sent to, but she didn't seem to remember exactly where it was. She described a 'high railed fence and big garden', but said that the girls were worked hard and not allowed to go out. She was obviously very unhappy there, and did not have visitors.

It was therefore very interesting to meet a lovely lady who had actually been a young mother in the Mrs Legge Home when it had moved to Tettenhall Road in the sixties. She was very brave in revealing to me a situation which was very hard for her to relate, as what she experienced, even now (over fifty years later) was something she has never recovered from. Naturally her memories were extremely emotional but, she did relate a lot to me about life in the home at that time, and considering how strict it was then made us realise it had probably been much worse thirty years and earlier when, of course, the girls knew even less.

It seems there were different regimes for the mums-to-be and the mums who had delivered their babies. The mums-to-be had certain work to do to ensure the smooth running of the home for everyone, which included doing the household laundry, all the babies' nappies (washed and rinsed in cold water), the cleaning of the house and floors, ironing, making or knitting baby clothes and general work. Meals were, however, prepared by kitchen staff. The mums-to-be shared bedrooms and similarly the girls who had become mothers shared bedrooms in a different part of the house, and were responsible for the care of their baby until such time as they either left, taking the baby with them, or when the baby went for foster care or adoption. The girls who had given birth were therefore taken off the household duties at that time.

When a girl entered the home she had to take with her certain items of necessity for her unborn child, such as terry towelling nappies, tiny nightdresses, jackets and toiletries. The girls knitted small garments during the months awaiting the arrival of their babies. The nappies had to be either embroidered or marked so that the laundry knew to whom they belonged, and it seems the girls were not advised of what would happen during the birth, although they did receive some pre-natal care. It is not known if any pre-natal care was given in the original home on North Road.

When the girls entered the home they had to go through some very intimate and embarrassing physical examinations to ensure the girls were 'free of disease', and it is possible this would have been even more stringent in the early years of the home on North Road from 1915, through the years my birth mother was there in the 1940s and on into the 1960s. Certainly young girls like my birth mother knew very little about pregnancy and birth (or even how babies were conceived), so it must have been extremely traumatic to endure such privations. I was told some horrendous stories about medical staff which I am not prepared to reveal here. After all, these were not 'bad' girls, and were only accepted into the home being 'first time offenders', as it was put!

Obviously, the girls would help each other and form friendships to have a little fun, but at North Road only one visitor was allowed and that visitor had to sit at the end of the long dining table whilst the girls sat at the other. No hugs or contact with the visitor was permitted. However I suspect that life in the sixties was a little more lenient than previously, as the girls there did manage to go out occasionally.

Of course some babies were actually born at 89 North Road, and probably also at 134 Tettenhall Road, where it is to be hoped the girls would feel more comfortable, but for those who had to go to hospital it is understandable they felt very frightened and alone as frequently staff made it quite clear that the lack of a wedding ring told its own story, and their attitude could be very patronising. It is to be hoped that not all nursing staff were like that; surely there were some comforting ones, although these single mothers were most definitely not accepted or kindly treated as they are today!

When the girls returned to the Mrs Legge Home as mothers they entered into a very different routine. Now the girl was responsible for the care of her child, and for the first eight weeks of the baby's life it would join other babies in the nursery. The mothers were not allowed to breastfeed or cuddle their babies so as to prevent a bond developing prior to the adoptive parents taking their new family away. The baby was bottle-fed by its mother whilst lying in its cot, and visits were on a strict four-hourly feeding and changing routine. However, Mother Nature tends to overcome such rules and many mothers, naturally, were overwhelmed with their maternal feelings for their little one. The babies were put

The Rake and Pikel where my birth parents met.

outside to 'take the air' every day, come hail, storm or freezing weather. It seems there was quite a rush at those times to try and get the least dilapidated pram in which to put their baby. With the home being a charitable institution, it would seem most of their equipment had been donated, thus resulting in an eclectic mixture of items. The girls were not allowed to push their babies around in the prams, even though there was a large garden at the rear of the property. They simply had to place the baby in a pram and leave it tucked up there to get fresh air.

Adoption day was the Waterloo for many of these poor girls, who had no choice but to let their baby go for adoption. Normally a social worker would give the new mother a fortnight's warning that the baby was to be collected by its new parents, so the girl could put together a 'Welcome Box' to be presented to the adoptive parents. All the embroidery or stitching on the nappies for identification had to be unpicked, and the nappies placed in the box together with the child's toiletries, nighties and little knitted garments made during the waiting period. Apparently it was routine at Tettenhall Road for a photograph of the baby to be taken before the new parents arrived to be given to the natural mother, but it is not known if the same applied to North Road, as photography was far rarer at that time, and very expensive. The lady I met told me she took great care with her box, wrapping it in cellophane, but she kept a small pair of bootees her baby had worn and which she still treasures to this day.

The babies were given their last feed on adoption day by their mother, and collections usually took place at 2 p.m. so that the baby could be in its new home in time for the next four-hourly feed. For an hour after the baby had been taken from its mother the girl had to stay alone in a room – probably to allow the paperwork to be completed and the adoptive parents to take the baby away without the mother seeing them. Otherwise they would probably have had screaming girls running down the road after the babies! It sounds so cruel that these things happened, but as we now know from television programmes and films, they did this all over the country in similar homes and institutions.

Vera, when I had asked about her personal experience, told me that she was very frightened in hospital as she had no idea what was going to happen. Her own mother went to see her after I was born and when she told her mother about the pain of childbirth, the response was 'Well, that's what happens to naughty girls!'

Although the regime of the Mrs Legge Home sounds horrifying in this day and age, at least it did give unmarried girls a place to deliver their babies, and probably saved many lives. Otherwise, where could they have gone? At the time I can remember it was such a disgrace for any family to discover their neighbours knew about a 'fallen daughter', and if families refused to let a girl stay at home and there was no one else or no other member of the family where they could be sent, she would finish up destitute, on the streets or in the workhouse, which would have been infinitely worse!

The girls who entered the Mrs Legge Home were branded, as we have discovered, 'first-time offenders'. If that can be taken as a true description, then most of them came from good families who had, themselves, to pay for the girl's care whilst in the home. Sometimes girls did return to partners, who were the fathers, and experienced a happy marriage and family life, or later married someone who was happy to take their child on as their own. Indeed, some babies were sent for fostering upon leaving the Mrs Legge Home, but later reclaimed by their birth mother once she had a settled life and family home.

However, as I can personally confirm, many of these girls never, for the rest of their lives, got over their experiences in such homes or, indeed, being deprived and forcibly parted from their baby. We see this now on television in such programmes as *Long Lost Family* and *Who Do You Think You Are*, and despite some people being sceptical about the truthfulness of those stories they are, in fact, quite true! It made me really wonder so much what had happened to Vera after she left the Mrs Legge Home, and raised even more questions about where I had gone! It seems she went back home to Saighton and took me with her; I would have been between two and three months old then. Mrs Legge, for the times, was very far-seeing, and must have been a very compassionate and understanding woman regarding these girls. She obviously did the very best she could for them in view of the general attitude that the girls were always the ones at fault!

It must have been traumatic for Vera, too, and I can well understand the story Auntie Betty tells me. She remembers that during the days when I was taken back to the family home in Saighton for a very short time Vera sat in a 'trance' at the side of the fire. My aunt had never really understood what her sister had gone through until she heard of how life must have been for her before and after my birth. These 'things' were never discussed with the rest of the family in those days.

At the time of my birth Auntie Betty would have been seventeen, about to marry and had moved to the West Midlands, but she obviously did know about my existence. Joan, the eldest sister, was married and living a distance away, and the boys still at home were fifteen, thirteen and eleven. Such a busy farming family would not have been able to keep permanent attendance on Vera and a small baby, and obviously with Vera's serious epilepsy she could not be left alone with a tiny baby for safety reasons. She could suffer multiple seizures in a day. My birth father was not around, so Vera could not marry. It is very tragic to realise the situation, and whatever came next it is obvious that she had never recovered from her serious accident when she was burnt at the age of fourteen to fifteen, and now her first baby was to be taken away from her.

From the family home it would appear that Vera's older sister, Joan, took me to Cheshire County Council to be placed for fostering. It seems my aunt had especially gone into Chester to purchase a shawl to wrap me in for this occasion and Auntie Betty had told me that my grandmother, herself and Joan cried a lot when I was finally put in the care of Cheshire County Council for fostering.

The sad thing is that Joan died at the age of forty-seven, and she was the one person who would have carried information about what had actually happened when Vera was pregnant, sent away, returned and how decisions were made about my welfare. Also, I realised that my grandparents, too, were deceased. They would have been very informative if I had ever had the opportunity and they had agreed to meet me.

It took almost three years to assemble all the information about the Mrs Legge Home, and once completed in March 2015 I put together a small booklet complete with relevant photographs and presented the same, as promised, to the Archives and Central Library in Wolverhampton. I was amazed during that year how many people wished to have copies of this booklet. Both newspapers had printed articles about the booklet, so I received requests from as far away as Australia and many from the length and breadth of the UK for people who, like me, had always wished to know what or where 89 North Road was. One gentleman aged ninety-two had been born at 89 North Road, and he was so thrilled at long last to discover information about his birthplace. It made my efforts so worthwhile.

So, in March 2015 I thought my endeavours were complete and that it was time to settle down properly and get involved in other things.

CHAPTER 16

Moving Forward

The years between 2012 and 2015 were quite incredible in themselves, and life moved forward very quickly and positively. A slow start and then it was almost like a rolling-stone, gathering events, possibilities and recovery in its wake.

I had always loved travelling, and through Jenny and Gill, my new friends, I began slowly to commence some journeys once more. Initially in 2009 whilst Gerald was still in care, Maureen and I were invited to accompany them on some of their 'lochs and glens' trips – just a week's holiday, usually in January or February – and for a few years we did just that. I had been very dubious about leaving Gerald at first in 2009, but they reassured me he would be in good hands whilst I was away and it would also give me something to tell him about on my return. I did enjoy the short break, though it was overshadowed with telephone calls to ensure Gerald was all right, and he was always at the back of my mind, of course. For four years we visited different areas in Scotland and they were a happy interlude in between the worry and anguish about what was happening at home.

After Gerald's passing in 2010 I shared a trip with my friend Beryl to Majorca, which in some ways made up for what had happened when we were in Morocco, and then in 2011 I felt it was time to take another 'just you' holiday and begin to make an attempt at living again.

I chose a 'Classic Cities of Italy' trip this time, one of the places we stopped being Sorrento, which brought back both happy and sad memories of Ian as that was the first trip abroad we had taken. Still, it was a wonderful trip with a lovely group of people and although I did not realise it at the time something absolutely amazing was about to happen beyond my wildest dreams.

Looking back at my video film of this trip I had noticed one person who always seemed to be at the back of the group. It was a man I cannot particularly remember talking to very much, but he was obviously very observant. On the aircraft flying back home I found him sitting next to me, and we made pleasant conversation. He introduced himself as John and we discussed the holiday we had just experienced.

John was very interested in aircraft and in our conversation I had mentioned Cosford Air Museum, which is under half an hour away from where I live. He said he had always wished to visit this museum and asked me if we could meet one Sunday perhaps, and I could take him there. I agreed, and a few weeks later after meeting for lunch at a local restaurant he followed me in his car up to Cosford. I was very impressed with his knowledge of the antique aircraft, and it was almost like having a 'personal' guide, which made it even more interesting.

Over the next few months we met up for a few trips out here and there – John lived 50 miles away in Leicestershire, but like myself he was interested in history and museums so we visited various places either near myself or his home. He thought Ironbridge was fascinating, and it was nice to have company. Naturally I had told him about Gerald and made it quite clear I was not looking for any relationships apart from companionship. He felt the same, so I did not worry too much about the situation and just enjoyed the odd visits to places.

In 2012 we were having lunch before visiting a museum when John made me an offer. He told me he had always loved travelling and wished to continue to do so. As he was a few years older than myself, he made it clear he did not wish to travel alone any more, and had been hoping to meet someone who could be a travelling companion, and asked if I was interested. I was not too sure how to take this at first, but he told me about a cruise he had seen on offer to Croatia and Dubrovnik and asked if I liked cruises. I had only experienced the small cruise with Ian many years ago, but I remembered how lovely that was (apart from my injuries of course). That had been with my husband, though, and this was not the same situation, although John was a very pleasant man!

I gently explained to John that cruises were way beyond my pocket these days, being a widow on my own, and he told me this was not an issue. He wanted a travelling companion who was interested in the same things he was, and after our outings over the past few months he had got to know me better and felt I might enjoy some travels as his 'companion'. All he asked was that I would pay my own way for trips out, anything I wished to buy, drinks etc. So, that was the offer. I did not drink or smoke, which were major considerations for John, and I suspect that on the Classic Italy trip he had been watching for someone suitable to make this offer to, so he would not be travelling alone as he got older.

I wanted to think very carefully about this, but it was a bit like déjà vu from the time Gerald and I had met each other when he had suggested we meet up, and it felt quite weird. Once again, I told Margaret, Helen and my friends what had been offered and I got similar reactions – 'Go for it', 'If you are not happy, it's only a week and you don't need to go again', 'Wow, if you don't want to go I will', and 'What have you got to lose? It could be a marvellous experience', and suchlike.

So, throwing all my eggs into the basket I agreed to go, and it turned out to be wonderful. I thoroughly enjoyed the cruise – a much bigger ship this time, the Norwegian Cruise Line – and of course the trips onshore were brilliant and I never felt threatened in any way whatsoever. John was a good companion, kept himself to himself, was clean and tidy and

My love of history, archaelogy and travelling.

when I asked if I could go to the cinema on the ship (he doesn't care for cinemas), he told me this was a democracy and it was my holiday just the same as his.

He was so generous in taking this attitude and over the coming years I lost count of how many cruises and trips we took together. I always made a video disc for him of our holidays so in effect he had the whole trip there to watch over again whenever he wished, and we went further and further afield.

In 2013 we did the 'Top to Toe of Italy' (a land tour), Malta and a cruise from Australia to Hong Kong, taking in Bali and Vietnam.

In 2014 We had two big cruises – one to Hawaii, Samoa and Tahiti, and the other a South Pacific cruise taking in Australia, New Zealand and Fiji. We also did the parks and canyons of America which was incredible, and during which I made some good friends who live in Nottingham. This was a coach trip, and remains one of the most wonderful experiences of travelling I have ever known.

2015 brought trips to Paris and Versailles, followed by New Zealand. We also visited the D-Day beaches in 2015 –after which nothing would ever be the same again, knowing what was discovered there, but I will cover that later.

We had a Caribbean cruise and a tour to Boston, New York and Washington in 2016, also later on taking a fortnight's touring holiday of Ireland at that time, driving from north to south.

The French Riviera was one of the venues for 2017, together with a holiday on the Algarve, and then in 2018 we took a Baltic cruise and a never-to-be-forgotten trip to India, which included a visit to the Taj Mahal.

These visits probably do not cover everywhere we went in those years, and I know John hopes to do even more, providing health and ability allow. John has never been married and has no dependants, and so travel has been the main thing for him since he retired, and in a way I feel very glad that I have enabled him in some ways to do this, as he would not have gone on his own any more. He had travelled extensively himself, probably circumnavigating the world a couple of times in the past, but certainly there is not much fun taking trips alone, as it is always nice to have someone to discuss things with, and it gives more of a feeling of security as we reach later years.

Not being happy in cold weather conditions, John usually rents an apartment somewhere in Spain for two or three months of the year from November through to around March, unless a trip is planned of course, and I can't say I blame him.

Suffice to say, John has obviously been a very good friend over these years and as I made it crystal clear at the start of our friendship that I was not looking for a partnership of any sort I think he was glad about that, and the understanding has allowed us the freedom of simply a thoroughly good companionship.

For myself, I find it totally unbelievable that such an

opportunity presented itself to me at all, particularly after some very tough years. I cannot help wondering if Ian and Gerald are sitting on a little pink cloud together somewhere and have organised this for me in some way, knowing how I loved to travel and that I would be perfectly safe with John. That may sound completely idiotic, but who knows? Had the roles been reversed I would have wished the same opportunities for them, but they lost their lives far too soon, as Ian was only sixty-four and Gerald was of a similar age to Ian when he too passed away. It certainly makes one realise how precious life is and that we need to take every single opportunity that comes our way. I am so thankful I did, and could never repay John for the wonderful experiences he has opened to me and, I hope, will continue to do so for some time yet to come.

When life seems to settle down and become somewhat normal again, it is then that surprising things tend to happen. I really thought that the 'jigsaw' of my life was almost complete in 2015, as I knew there were obviously many things which would never be solved or discovered, particularly about my birth father, but after my donation of the booklet in March 2015 life seemed to have settled down nicely. I had been on some fabulous worldwide trips by that time and thirty-six copies of my booklet had been distributed to people who wanted one as far away as Australia, so it felt as if I had done something really useful, for once. There couldn't be anything further to discover, could there? I knew about my half-brother and sister in Ireland and was still in touch with Carolyn of course, so really the lid on Pandora's Box was closing.

Oh no it wasn't!

CHAPTER 17

You Couldn't Make it Up!

———

John and I returned from a lovely fortnight in Lanzarote in February 2015, and as is usual when one feels energetic upon returning from such a trip I decided to sort out a large wicker basket of papers in my loft which had been there since Gerald was taken ill.

Now, over the previous four or five years I never stopped wondering about my birth family, but having made a few discoveries there did not seem to be any way forward. I had written letters to Cheshire County Council on several occasions attempting to find some care papers relating to myself, which had always finished up with a definite reply of 'there is nothing now – old fostering papers would have been destroyed'.

This seemed rather presumptive, as up until that time, at the age of sixty-seven, it made me feel as if I was really a 'displaced' person with no legal or definite evidence that my birth and marriage certificates related to the same person, albeit with backup of the statutory declaration I had sworn. In substance, I could have disappeared to another country, started another life, committed bigamy – and no one would have been any the wiser. I could have disappeared, literally. Something deep inside told me there just *had* to be something, somewhere, relating to me. Even medical papers cannot be destroyed until people pass away, so the birth of a child and what happened to it must have been on record somewhere.

Mum and Gran would have had some legal papers relating

to my fostering, which had probably been destroyed when I was around sixteen or eighteen years of age, as they would not have wished me to read anything like that. As far as they were concerned, the situation had never existed at all. They would never have understood the need for me, as a person, wishing to know where I came from, who my birth family were or what had happened to me. I had great respect for the way they felt, and always have, but the doubts just never went away.

I have since wondered what Mum and Gran were told on the occasions Miss Bissett-Smith visited them in the 'inner sanctum' at home. As I have said before, I only have actual recollections of her visiting two or three times at the most, but she must have made more regular visits as I now know that Cheshire County Council were my guardians, not my mum and/or gran. Each time she visited them over a period of ten years she must have advised them of whatever information she knew about Vera, so as the years went by they probably knew an awful lot, but destroyed whatever evidence that information contained.

The only positive link I had ever encountered was that little piece of blue paper which had names, addresses and dates written on it, and which I had stupidly lost during three house moves. Why had I been so careless with such a precious item? It was a sickening thought that a simple piece of notepaper with my mum's handwriting on it could have been the key to goodness knows what. And now it was too late.

John and I had planned a trip to visit the D-Day beaches in France later in the year, which is somewhere I had always wished to visit, particularly as my dad had been in the D-Day landings. The trip was to commence on the 2nd of August for four days, and was something we were really looking forward to. So, in the four months leading up to the trip following the completion of my booklet about the Mrs Legge Home I had started to put many things in order around my flat which I had never had the heart to do following Gerald's loss.

On a rainy day in July 2015 I decided it was high time to shred a lot of the obsolete papers contained in the aforesaid wicker hamper, so armed with a large bin bag I sat on the loft floor and went through its contents. It was a rather uncomfortable situation as the loft is not high enough to stand or even sit on a chair. I was about to give up and take a lot of old papers which were out of date downstairs to shred, and was about to close the basket lid when I saw a tiny corner of blue paper. No – it couldn't be, could it? Things don't happen like that. I grasped it and pulled – and yes, it was! The very piece of paper which had been missing for so long! I just knelt there staring at it, not believing how it had suddenly reappeared. Was it fate, knowing it was the 'right' time?

The former letters I had sent to Cheshire County Council had simply contained information I could remember from the time my mum had died, but here in front of me were the actual addresses and relevant dates when I had been taken to these places! Because I had initially mislaid the paper I had been unable to furnish dates to the council in my more recent letters, but here they were once again! I was obviously still in Wolverhampton with Vera at 89 North Road at the age of one month, as I was registered in Wolverhampton, and then more than likely in the next month or so when Vera left the home I would have been taken back to the family home at Saighton for a short time, which Auntie Betty had confirmed. I was then taken to 4 Wilton Street, Wallasey at the age of three months (probably to a children's home), and then at eight months put into Kilrie Children's Home in Knutsford, Cheshire where I remained until Mum (with, possibly, Gran) took me out of there at the age of twenty months and became my foster parents! I was then taken to my first 'real' home at 75 Castleway, Pendleton, Salford 6.

I knew of course that we had moved from Pendleton to Charlesworth in Derbyshire, quite a distance away from Salford, on the other side of Manchester completely, and once

The house in Saighton where I was taken for a very short time around 2 months old.

more felt this could well have been that Mum and Gran did not wish neighbours to know anything at all. They would not have told any 'outsider' their business, but it would have been obvious they would have known something anyway with a twenty-month-old child suddenly appearing out of nowhere! I have a very misty recollection of Castleway and do definitely remember a lady handing me a banana over the hedge – this possibly stuck in my 'baby mind' because I had more than probably just been transferred from Kilrie Home to Castleway: a huge changeover in people and surroundings which I would have been acutely aware of, even at that young age.

I also know we lived in Charlesworth until I was around five years old, so the reason for the move to Hyde must have been because I was to start school. I do remember going to nursery school in Charlesworth and learning a poem which Dad used to tease me about.

It could never be explained how fabulous the discovery of this small piece of blue paper was to me. Not only did it reveal just where I had spent the first twenty months of my life, but it meant little bits of the unsolved jigsaw were once more being put in place. So, where did I go from here?

On a complete gamble I then decided to write *once* more to Cheshire County Council, giving the addresses and relevant dates, to see if they might help trace some papers relating to me – after all it was the most definite bit of information I had ever found. I can't say I held out much hope really, but busied myself preparing for the trip to the D-Day beaches and didn't really give it much more thought for two or three weeks. I really thought it would be another 'red herring' and that I would receive the same replies as before – negative thoughts!

However, just a week before the trip I received a telephone call from a lovely lady called Julie, who worked at Cheshire West. She advised me that my letter had been forwarded to her, and that Chester Council had been split into two sections some time before; Cheshire West and Cheshire East. That could have explained why my previous letters did not reach the appropriate place, as Julie told me that Kilrie Children's Home came under Cheshire West, for whom she worked. She went on to tell me that she had found some papers relating to me – not many, but if I could prove who I was she would send them to me! This literally took my breath away.

This was not only unbelievable, but rather odd, as of course those papers were what I needed to prove my identity, so all I could do was tell her about the statutory declaration. She was quite happy with that, and told me she would eagerly await my confirmation, birth and marriage certificates. However, at this time she was not able to tell me anything which was in those papers. I just couldn't believe this – I had waited sixty-seven years for someone to actually tell me I existed! Wow.

Upon receipt of my documentation, Julie telephoned me back and said she had sent the care papers to me by recorded delivery, as they contained 'sensitive personal information'. They were due to arrive just two days before I went away, and I have to admit many emotions went through me at the prospect of receiving these documents, which I still couldn't believe had been found after all that time. Julie had said there were not many papers – only eighteen pages. Eighteen pages? Goodness me – far more than I could ever have expected! She also told me that I may have a few 'surprises' when I received the papers. What on earth could that mean?

I soon found out. The papers arrived the day before I left on my holiday, and to this day I cannot remember one moment of the journey down the M6 to Leicestershire that morning to collect my travelling companion, John, as my mind was in an absolute whirl. What I had discovered was going round and round and round and it was difficult to take it all in. Actually, it took some time to come to terms with the information I had received.

I had known about my half-brother and sister, Robert and Carolyn, since 1995, as Vera had told me about them. However, she had said that they had died as babies with their father in a house fire, which I had discovered for myself was untrue. What she had *not* revealed to me was that there were *three* more children born to her in between myself, Robert and Carolyn. So, I had been the eldest of six children! SIX children?

Having been brought up as an only child, I just could not take this in. I had been born in 1948, I had a sister Hazel born in 1950, another sister called Vera born in 1952 and a brother called Robert born in 1954. Vera had then given birth to a second boy she called Robert in 1957, married his father, moved to Ireland and then gave birth to Carolyn in 1959. So, she had six children in a period of eleven years.

Why Vera had two sons called 'Robert' was quite strange. All I could conclude was that she may not have told her husband about the previous four births, and when their son was born the father wished the child to be named after him, who was also a 'Robert'. Who knows?

I had a wonderful holiday visiting the D-Day beaches, which really took my thoughts for a while off the mind-blowing information I had just received, but upon returning home it all crowded in and I just could not believe any of it. Where were they all? What had happened to them? Were they still alive? Did they know about me? Had my mum and Gran known about these other children? Vera had certainly kept some big secrets very close to her – and fancy telling me her two youngest had died as babies! What was it all about – had she genuinely forgotten giving birth to all these children, or was it selective memory? I shall never know. I suspect Mum and Gran also were very good at keeping 'secrets'. It was like something out of a novel!

All I could gather from my personal papers was that the first four of us had all been illegitimate and probably all born to different fathers. Three of us had been fostered out but Vera (the third child) had actually been adopted. There were quite a lot of remarks from social services in my papers which I could not believe – had these comments been written in this day and age it would have been completely unacceptable. It was clear, however, that social services were most definitely *not* enamoured with Vera or her lifestyle in general, but it seemed awful to me that she must have lost every single baby she gave birth to – all six of us. That was a very tragic situation indeed.

I hoped my brothers and sisters had all received a good home and upbringing, and now I guess I had to try and discover where they were and what had happened to them. That wooden spoon was *still* stirring rapidly!

I also gathered from my papers that my birth mother, Vera, had been mentally unstable, and that the children were most likely taken off her because of her epilepsy, which is so sad. The family doctor who had known Vera from childhood had not considered that her first baby (me) should have been taken off her. My daughters and I discussed things at length, and we all felt that Vera had really suffered a tragic life after being badly burnt at the age of fourteen and hospitalised until she was fifteen – probably undergoing skin grafts, and then losing her first baby, experiencing the trauma of being in the Mrs Legge Home away from her family to have me, and then upon returning home having to allow her sister, Joan, to take me to Chester County Council for fostering. No wonder the poor woman sat in a 'trance' at the side of the fire at home that time! It sounded as if she was completely traumatised.

So, now I had these papers, what was the next step? I telephoned Julie at Cheshire West, who was as helpful and pleasant as she was allowed to be, but she told me that although Hazel's and Robert's files were also there, she was unable because of current legislation to tell me what was in them. Vera's file was not with Cheshire West, as she explained this would have been sent to the relevant court when the child was adopted. All she could tell me was that Hazel had given birth to_ten children, that Robert had a disability and that it was possible Hazel had lived in the Liverpool area. Ten children? My nephews and nieces!

My daughters were as amazed as I was at the contents of my papers, but it was so fascinating to read the records of my first year, how I grew and developed, the knowledge that somewhere out in the big wide world were a lot of relatives I had never known even existed, and now what to do about it?

The story Dad told me about his returning from work to find me playing on the rug without his knowledge was also true. The only person who took me out of Kilrie Home was my mum. Hers was the only name on the Kilrie papers. This did not really seem feasible, as surely the entire family would have been vetted, as would the home at Castleway, but of course post-war there were thousands of illegitimate babies to be fostered out and perhaps the family scrutiny for fostering was not as thorough as adoption would have been. I still wondered if Gran had signed any papers on behalf of Dad. I wouldn't have put it past her!

I discovered that in 1954, when I was six years old, I was actually put up for adoption, but for reasons unknown to me it never went through. Perhaps this was a financial situation, which I understand, as fostering payments would have ceased to Mum and Gran had an adoption gone through, but it didn't mean they thought any the less of me. When I had asked Vera why I had not been adopted she said it had been because she would not sign the relevant papers, but obviously that was also untrue.

There was a note in the file that my birth mother had 'visited me' in 1961 when I would have been thirteen, but this definitely did not happen when I was around as I would have remembered such an event. If the social worker had turned up at our house with my birth mother I doubt very much if they would have even been allowed over the doorstep, taking into account my Mum and Gran's wrath at such a possibility. It did, however, make me wonder if it was true, and whether it was the reason we moved so quickly up to Mottram when I was fourteen. Dad had not wished to move as it would make his travelling to work so much more difficult and distant, but it was taken out of his hands. Had Vera turned up and this was a true event, I imagine that could well have been the reason Mum and Gran wished to get away from an address my birth mother would have now been aware of!

My care notes ended in 1964 when I turned sixteen, but the records had been updated until then with the changes of address from Salford, to Charlesworth in Derbyshire, to Hyde in Cheshire and finally to Mottram where we moved when I was fourteen.

At the time I was placed for adoption, it seems that Vera was asked about my birth father and did actually give a name, but this was also untrue. When social services had queried her about this she had referred to her fits and said she could not remember, but when a random name was produced to her she replied, 'You wouldn't be far wrong at that!' She also denied I had been born in Wolverhampton and insisted that *all four* of her babies were born in Chester. This does lead me to wonder if she had undergone some electric-shock therapy for her epilepsy in the six years since I was born, which could have genuinely wiped out some of her memory, and would also explain other things. I do also realise that she suddenly remembered she *had* given birth to four children at that time! One can only feel very sad for her but maybe there would be more to discover in the future regarding this.

Everything seemed to be a complete maelstrom of illogical contradiction and lack of communication all along the line, also some carelessness about filling in those care papers, which was done by hand in the 1940s. There was at least one big error in my birth date on one of the pages, so was the 'convenient' father's name also wrong? I think so, as I obtained further evidence at a later date which would have precluded the person named and also errors in other siblings' papers, too.

So – what was the next step? There were brothers and sisters, nephews and nieces unknown to me out there somewhere, living their lives just as I was without knowledge of each other. It must have been weeks before I really came down to earth and started to realise what I had discovered, and all I knew about my sister Hazel's family was that she had ten children who would now all be grown up. Hazel would be sixty-six, Vera sixty-four and Robert sixty-two. A lifetime spent apart.

The only information that Julie at Cheshire West had actually given me regarding Hazel was her surname, so it followed that her sons would still have that name. She had also told me that 'someone' had tried to find me! This became even more bizarre. Whoever had tried to trace me would never have been able to of course, as my birth and marriage certificates had never matched, so Judith Ashton had never married.

Years before, when attempting to find out if Robert (the second one, born in Ireland) and Carolyn were still alive, I had inserted an advertisement in the local paper, which had produced a positive and rapid outcome, so I decided on another of my impulses to do the same with this situation. I therefore telephoned the *Liverpool Echo* (quite a risk really) and explained the situation, gave a box number and email address and waited to see if anything happened, which I didn't really think would!

With regard to Vera (the daughter and my sister), this was a non-starter as she had been adopted, which meant that a post-adoption company would have to be employed if she was to be found, and as Robert (fourth child) was in care somewhere, with a condition or conditions unknown, there was no starting point to finding him.

However, my advertisement regarding Hazel's family was placed in the Liverpool Echo the following Saturday, and believe it or not by 6 p.m. that day I had received three replies – one from Alan, advising me he was Hazel's third eldest and asking 'Is there a particular reason for the interest in our family, thanks?' One from Holly, Hazel's eldest granddaughter, and one from Kirstie, Hazel's second born, who replied '*I have tried looking for some of you for sooooo long I could cry …*'

You couldn't have made this up!

CHAPTER 18

The Way Forward

At this point in time a friend I had known since childhood and who lived in Mottram had asked me if I would give a talk about the 'lost family' I had discovered to the Ladies' Society I had belonged to for six years. This was the start of building a regular 'talk' to groups of ladies and my local history group in Wolverhampton because of the booklet I had written regarding the Mrs Legge Home and my own story, and it had progressed over the four years since my donating the booklet to the Archives and library. I was amazed at how interested people were, and found myself having to return to various groups to give them 'updates' when I discovered more about my unusual revelations as the years progressed! This last 'update' after discovering my care papers was extremely fascinating! Quite a lot of groups wanted these talks, and they raised some nice little donations for my local hospice.

Following the amazing realisation that I had discovered the family of a sister born just twenty months after myself was quite something, and to then discover that she had a family of ten children was even more mind-blowing! My niece, Kirstie, became my first point of contact, and it was hard for her, too, to realise that her mother's older sister had been found after all hope had been given up!

It was not long before Kirstie and I started speaking to each other on the telephone, and in order to help her and the large family – many of whom were also interested – I compiled a file detailing what I knew about my own life and how I had discovered our birth mother, Vera. This file went around the entire family I believe, and hopefully it assisted them in getting to grips with what was, in effect, a stranger's lifetime enquiries. I also included what I knew about Vera, which at that time wasn't really a great deal. There were still so many irregularities and questions to be asked.

Kirstie told me that, sadly, her mother Hazel had died eighteen years earlier and she told me that it was following the loss of her mum that she herself was curious and had tried hard to find me. Of course, this would have been completely impossible as my birth name of Judith Ashton was not on my marriage certificate, and as the name had never been legally changed to that of my 'maiden' name there was no documentation which could have put Kirstie on the right track. Sadly, Hazel had been unaware that she had an older sister called Judith and also a younger sister called Vera. However, she did know about our brother Robert, as she had some memories of her own regarding him since childhood. When we first started to talk to each other Kirstie asked me if I

My beautiful sister Hazel. It was too late for us to meet!

knew anything about the missing sisters or brother and was quite amazed when I told her it was only the previous August, three or four months earlier, that I had discovered any of them even existed!

Kirstie was determined to acquire Hazel's care papers after Hazel had passed, but it was a real struggle and seemed for a long time she would not be allowed to have them. However her resolute willpower paid off and she did eventually acquire them. They followed much the same line as my own, although Hazel was fostered by Mr and Mrs Heller during her first few months then returned to a home (name unknown), but taken back by Mr and Mrs Heller at three years old. It was sad when Kirstie told me that her mum had 'never felt she belonged', which was such a shame, but I know that Hazel loved her parents Mr and Mrs Heller very much. It would have been so wonderful if we two sisters could have been brought up together as children, being so close in age – or even actually just known each other! By the time I discovered Hazel's existence it was far too late.

I told Kirstie about Robert and Carolyn in Ireland, and we shared the same query about there being 'two' Roberts – one born only three years after the other. Kirstie agreed with me that maybe Vera's husband, whom she married between 1986 and 1987, was also called Robert and wished his firstborn son to carry his name. We shall never know, but it does seem rather strange. I know it is reiterating what I have said before, but did Vera, in fact, tell her husband about the previous four children or that something had happened to them, or had she prevaricated about how she had lost them?

It was not long before Kirstie told me the names of Hazel's ten children – Michael, Kirstie, Alan, David, Jeanette, Kevin, Paul, Dale, Laura and Daniel. Eight of the children had been born to Hazel's first marriage, and the youngest two when she remarried.

I had also advised Carolyn that she had more sisters and

another brother, and she was as confounded as myself. It was very exciting, but in some ways there was underlying sadness that we had all lived our lives without knowing anything about each other. Kirstie felt that Hazel would have been very interested and, like myself, completely dumbfounded at our unexpected discoveries.

We could not wait to meet up, and so after Christmas 2015, just five months after discovering Kirstie and Hazel's large family, Carolyn and I made arrangements for her to fly over to England to come and stay with me, so then we could meet up with our 'new' family of nephews and nieces together for the first time. This amazing meeting was arranged for the 20th of February 2016 and it was decided that Carolyn and I would drive over to Neston on the Wirral to meet everyone at the Royal Oak – which had a room large enough to accommodate us all! Kirstie had told me that all her brothers and sisters and their families still lived within a two-mile radius of each other!

What a loving and welcoming family they were. It was quite daunting to walk into a room full of strange faces, but we were soon put at our ease and presented with a magnificent bouquet of flowers each. Talk about the Tower of Babel! Everyone had so many questions, and of course it was impossible so soon to put names to faces, but how the time flew as we all shared a wonderful meal and exchanged what information we had. There were many family resemblances throughout the group.

Many photographs remain as a wonderful memory of that day, with the fun, laughter, chatter and inexplicable feelings – particularly for an only child to realise what a huge family she actually had! Carolyn and I met seven out ten of Hazel's children and we have remained in touch ever since. I visit Neston whenever I can as it is quite a distance for me to drive, and Kirstie and I remain in constant touch by telephone and messages.

Naturally we discussed the realisation that Hazel and I had

other half-siblings: Vera, who had been adopted, and Robert, who had probably been in care all of his life, and it was unknown where he was by now.

With regard to our missing sister, Vera, all we knew was that she had been adopted, and this was a difficult situation indeed as people are not allowed to trace adoptees. This takes a specialist company – as we know from *Long Lost Family* on television – who have permission and the ability to 'go beyond' the adoption files in order to trace people, so it seemed the only way we were going to discover anything about her would be to follow that path. I made a promise to set the wheels in motion as soon as possible to try to find Vera, but as it would be costly I had to wait a few more months to do so.

Kirstie remembered going to visit a gentleman called Robert with her mother, but of course she was only a child herself then and didn't really know the significance of this. He was, of course, the half-brother of myself, Hazel, Vera, Robert in Ireland and Carolyn.

Hazel's Story

Hazel was born on the 18th of October 1950, twenty-one months after myself, in Chester. According to Hazel's care papers it seems that due to our birth mother's frequent epileptic fits and it being necessary for one of our birth family to be constantly with her, they were unable to give continuous care for her and so Hazel was taken into care when only a couple of months old. She was initially fostered by Mr and Mrs Heller and then it would appear Mr and Mrs Bishop took her. However, Mr and Mrs Heller fostered Hazel once again from three years old and she lived with them until she married at the age of seventeen and believed them to have adopted her. She loved them very much and it was a happy home for her with her foster brothers. Kirstie tells me that her mother never felt she was really 'wanted', which may have stemmed from her belief she was adopted and therefore she probably wondered why our birth mother had abandoned her, which is something many fostered or adopted children feel. Hazel did not discover she was only fostered until she was seventeen, and so that news came as quite a shock. At that time Hazel was expecting her first baby and due to get married, so poor Mrs Heller was extremely worried about the effect this bombshell might have on Hazel.

Of course this situation now caused a few problems, as even though Mr and Mrs Heller were considered to be Hazel's parents, her birth mother's permission for Hazel to marry had to be sought despite the fact neither Hazel or Vera had ever had contact and were, literally, strangers to each other. However, the matter was resolved eventually and thankfully Hazel came to terms with the fostering rather than adoptive situation, as either way it did not change the parents who loved her and whom she loved as well as her brothers, who were Mr and Mrs Heller's 'natural' children. She had been brought up in a very happy home.

On Hazel's care papers it was noted prior to Hazel's marriage that our birth mother was incapable of giving consent to the marriage and it was also considered it might not be wise for Mrs Brownlee (Vera's married name) to know she had a married daughter, as they felt she might 'latch on' to her and make life quite impossible.

Vera (our birth mother) was by this time herself married, living in Ireland and it seems frequently needing medical care. This meant that only the permission of Hazel's guardian, the children's officer at Cheshire County Council, was required for Hazel to marry. The council actually gave Hazel and her fiancé £5 as a wedding gift for them to purchase cutlery with, which seemed very generous.

Hazel had been placed for adoption in September 1958, but like myself this situation did not go through so my sister also came up against the problem of being called by the family name of Heller during her upbringing. However, in her case she did not have to swear any statutory declarations as her foster parents would be signing her marriage certificate. I do wonder if that was 'tried on' with my mum and Gran too – it is possible! Never going to happen!

When Kirstie applied for, and eventually received, Hazel's care papers, the above situations became clearer to her and my name as her older sister was in those papers. Also mentioned was a paragraph stating that Hazel had a brother who was rather 'sub-normal'. That report was made in 1968. The two half-siblings in Ireland, Robert and Carolyn Brownlee, were also mentioned in Hazel's care papers. There was nothing in Hazel's care papers however about the third sister, Vera, who had been adopted, and so Hazel would never have known of her existence.

As mentioned previously, we knew Hazel had visited our brother Robert in Greaves Hall Hospital in Southport. I understand that one of the foster brothers brought up with Hazel knew of Robert being her true brother and advised Hazel of this at some point. Later on in life Hazel received a visit from someone in authority who actually advised her where Robert was, and must have been such a lovely person as she went to see and continued to visit him until she herself was too ill to attend any more. Kirstie believes she was around thirteen when she accompanied her mother to Greaves Hall, so Robert would have been in his thirties at that time.

This hospital has since been demolished, but Kirstie remembers her mother saying that Robert was simply in a dayroom left to his own devices more or less, and was with young adults from around twenty years upwards who all had Down Syndrome. There was no interaction between them and seemingly no effort to help them progress. As Robert did not have Down Syndrome, it would appear he was simply placed there because there was nowhere else he could go at that time. Someone did state they believed he had suffered a severe epileptic seizure at around the age of eight which had caused his disability, but this later turned out to be quite untrue: Robert never had such a seizure.

Following the loss of Hazel, Kirstie has no idea where Robert was directed after leaving the hospital in Southport, although she has a couple of ideas, one of them being a placement at Great Sutton. This meant that when I met Kirstie and the family in Neston we immediately wished to try to discover where our brother was. Things were turning out quite amazingly now – I not only had all the nephews and nieces in Neston but also a half-brother somewhere! The only thing we could do was to attempt to discover his whereabouts and see what we could find out, so another search was definitely on the cards.

Robert's Story

Sadly, very little is known about Robert's life previously to 2017 apart from the smattering of memories regarding our sister visiting him. He was Vera's fourth child. Obviously Kirstie and I wished to know if he was still alive, and if so what had happened to him, but although I did my best to discover just where he was this was a nightmare because of data protection issues. Telephone calls to various councils revealed nothing and still all we knew is where Kirstie thought he might have been looked after. We knew he was at home in Saighton with our birth mother, Vera, at the age of one month, as my care papers revealed that information, although our mother Vera knew he would eventually 'go away'. So he was obviously taken into care in the first few months of his life and it seems a Mrs Plevin was his foster mother for some time.

After writing some letters explaining the situation to Chester County Council, at last some light was shed on the situation and I was advised that he was still alive and in care, but they would not reveal to me where he was. This all led to further copious correspondence and eventually I received a telephone call from one of Robert's carers, who advised me he was living in Ellesmere Port and that after all my explanations about the unusual circumstances and revelations, Kirstie and I could visit our brother/uncle on an ad-hoc basis. Gosh, what a breakthrough at long last.

The first visit in 2016 was really strange for both Kirstie and I – we went together and it was an amazing feeling to see Robert and speak to him. He is very high on the autistic spectrum and unable to talk or communicate very well, but it was confirmed he had never suffered an epileptic seizure, so we don't know where that came from. To see this lovely, gentle person and realise that Robert never had a proper home, a mother or any family all his life until Kirstie and I found him and visited was dreadful. Had he been born fifty years later he would probably have received help early on in his childhood with his condition, which could have turned his life around, but it would appear he has been institutionalised all of his life.

Robert had been with these wonderful carers for almost fifteen years when I first met him, so I queried whether his care papers revealed anything about his past. This was an odd situation as we received no information at all, since his carers stated they had never had his care file and do not know anything about his childhood or the years since then. Of course he himself is unable to tell anyone, but he does say things which his carers do not understand and it is obvious that if they could obtain his file it would not only benefit Robert but also the people who look after him, as it would probably throw some light on what happened to him over his previous life. There is a huge void here where no one knows anything of Robert's whereabouts for around thirty or forty years, and we do hope that somehow we can trace some information. Once again this is a real battle, and unless his advocate or personal social worker can be found and apply for these papers it does not look as if any further information will ever be known about Robert's life, which is dreadful.

When Robert was first placed in his current home he was a very different person from the one we see today, and it is therefore obvious his experiences have been traumatic, to say the least. One cannot help wondering why his personal file did not accompany him from place to place during his adulthood, which would have helped his carers understand far more than they currently do. They think the world of Robert, and the joy on his carers' faces at him finally having half-siblings was very genuine. So, this is an ongoing situation in itself. Once again, lack of communication and consistency.

Kirstie and I visit Robert whenever we can, and as my youngest daughter Helen now lives in Chester she also visits when she is able. We have told his carers as much as we ourselves know, and they themselves are very keen for further information to be obtained. It would help him so much. He had a wonderful Christmas in 2017 with a family around for the first time in his life, with presents, photographs of his newly-discovered family and visitors, and it was a joy to see his face light up.

We were not really aware as to whether he did recognise us, but he seems content and happy in his current home with carers who really love him and look after him so well. He certainly recognises us now after a year has passed and there are family photographs in his apartment. His wonderful carers frequently talk to him about us and he will let me give him a hug and a kiss when I visit and he will come and speak to me down the phone occasionally, using my name, which is quite recognisable.

Bobby is a keen Frank Sinatra fan, and can sing word perfect 'My Way' and some other songs. Yes, there could be a lot yet to learn about our brother, Robert, and even with such a short time knowing him I am aware his speech has improved.

In order to differentiate the two brothers called Robert, we usually refer to the first Robert who is in care as 'Bobby', to avoid any mistakes.

Vera's Story

This now left the situation regarding the third child, Vera, who was actually legally adopted in 1952. The only course of action I could take in this connection was to employ and pay a specialist team in an attempt to find her. It was quite a difficult situation, as I did not know whether Vera would still be alive, whether she knew she was adopted and, in any event, if she was found and contacted if she would even wish to meet up with an unknown family. Lots of unanswered questions once more, but it had to be done! I felt that even if she did not want contact it was the right thing to at least give her the option and opportunity if she wished. That should be her choice.

I therefore instructed an after-adoption team who were based in Birmingham, and went for an initial interview to confirm and give evidence of who I was and generally relate the circumstances, which they found very interesting indeed! I paid the appropriate fee in 2016 and the matter was left in their hands.

Having travelled to Birmingham to meet the team it was a fairly long and involved process to explain and produce evidence that I wished to find my half-sister. These matters are not taken lightly, and of course it is essential that all parties are aware of the possible outcome and the responsibility of maybe causing upset and worry to someone else. I knew this from my own experiences when attempting to find Vera, my birth mother, and after a lengthy interview the team agreed to try and find my missing sister.

However they, too, found getting information or assistance from Cheshire West Council just as difficult as I had done, and Vera's file was not with them, as upon her adoption this would have been sent to the appropriate court who dealt with the matter at the time. Finding the whereabouts and acquisition of that file took eighteen months, during which time I had more or less given up of discovering anything further, but in November 2017 I received a telephone call from After Adoptions advising me that they considered they had found the whereabouts of our missing sister!

CHAPTER 19

Missing Pieces of the Jigsaw: Will They Ever be Found?

───

It was by now 2017 and it had become a rather bizarre time in my life when I began to think of how far things had progressed – how far I had come with my discoveries and with how much trepidation I had started out on this unbelievable journey over forty years ago to find out who I was! The whole thing was completely like a fairy tale no one could think was true, and I don't think this story could have even been made up. However, truth is very often stranger than fiction. And of course it is still unfolding – but I now knew just *who* I was and where I came from!

As I pondered upon the past sixty-nine years, it felt like someone else had experienced those first realisations when I was not aware of my status in life or who I was or where I came from. The shy, timid child who did not realise she was fostered rather than adopted until she reached her twenties, and then the unanswered questions, doubts, feelings of disloyalty and guilt which were the stumbling blocks of my enquiries taking so long. There were huge gaps from one big step to the next which, if I had only had the courage back then, could have resulted in my knowing in person at least the sister, Hazel, I had lost so early on.

Why did my mum and Gran have such a wretched idea that things had to be kept secret? That is something I have never been able to understand, for they obviously felt (and actually told me) it was nothing to do with me! Of course the timescale and Victorian outlook they had played a huge part in this, as in the 1940s and 1950s family business was kept well away from nosey neighbours or prying eyes. I still feel that, rather than being ashamed of taking an unwanted child and giving it a good home, they should have been proud. In our modern age it is shouted from the rooftops and celebrated, which is how it should have been. Still, up to a point I do understand, and it was probably their intention to protect me because of the stigma illegitimacy still held. Sadly, it was a misdirected and misjudged outlook. If only they had felt it right to tell me whatever they knew, which may not have been much, but my whole upbringing was such that I was kept in the dark about everything and had no right to thoughts of my own about anything and everything. That is what made my teenage and early twenties so hard so live through, if only they had realised it.

The other huge deception here for me was the fact they never told me any of the medical background of my birth mother, which could actually have been very dangerous. They obviously knew of her epilepsy, but things are unfolding which could (and do) affect quite a few of her descendants. In our modern day and age far more is understood about epilepsy and there are wonderful medications which help to absolutely control or at least minimise the awful seizures. Years ago the poor souls were treated in barbaric conditions and without any understanding whatsoever, which led to thousands of tragedies in workhouses and hospitals with their antiquated ideas. And I can't help wondering what (if any) medications were given to Vera to assist her. Auntie Betty did tell me that she took phenobarbitone which in the 1950s was probably the only known solution, but it must have had awful side-effects. Sufferers could also be given a dreadful electric-shock treatment which had severe side-effects so we do not know how much these matters actually affected Vera's mental and physical condition. One of her social workers put a note in a file stating that it was considered Vera may have wished to be pregnant such a lot because she did not suffer a seizure when she was pregnant. I do question this, as it seems a very high price indeed to pay for relief from seizures and then to leave unwanted babies behind! I do not believe that.

Mum and Gran were obviously aware of the fact that my birth mother was epileptic, and I now wonder (hindsight being a marvellous thing!) if that was the reason for them keeping me so quiet, away from people, disallowing any independence and preventing me from hearing or watching things which could have 'triggered' the condition in me? If that is the case, I do understand their concerns, but also their ignorance, which in turn made my early life so isolated and prevented me from having any understanding of the world outside the cocoon of home. They did their best, and I was very lucky indeed to have a grandmother and mother who – although not giving thought to many things and having no understanding of my character – did give me a secure and moral upbringing. My dad, of course, was the best there could have ever been. What a restricted life he led, too – for just short of sixty years!

By 2017 a family friend, David, had by now put together an ancestry file tracing back from my birth mother, Vera. He discovered my ancestry back to thirteen-times my great grandparents, dating back to 1585! It appears that the family had always lived and worked within a twenty-mile radius of Chester itself, taking in many of the surrounding rural villages and picturesque churches. I accompanied David on a day's outing to visit some of these places, and it was really weird to think that I was standing in the footsteps of my own ancestors. Again, quite unbelievable. So, from being an only child who knew absolutely nothing about myself, I now knew around four hundred years of my background! This, to me, was another amazing situation, for it confirmed my roots from Saighton 'big-time'!

My husband's family ancestry had always fascinated me, as Ian's was a long and fascinating story on his paternal side, as one of his aunts had discovered that he was the last of the direct-line of Robert Glover the Martyr, who is actually named in Foxe's Book of Martyrs! He was always so proud of this story. The family had originated from Baxterley, Atherstone and Mancetter in Warwickshire, living in the beautiful black and white Tudor Mancetter Manor for over a hundred years. Being staunch protestants, it was in the year 1555 at the height of the Marion Persecutions, that the order to bring the Glover family to trial was made.

There were three brothers: William, Robert and John. Upon hearing of the dangers, William and John fled; nothing was discovered really about what happened to them afterwards. However, Robert was ill in bed at Mancetter Manor when the sherriff's men forced their way into the Manor and dragged Robert from his sick bed and down the beautiful white oak staircase to be put on trial in Lichfield. He was found guilty, would not deny his faith, and on the 20th of September 1555, Robert Glover was burnt at the stake in Coventry. On a roundabout in modern-day Coventry there is a stone cross etched with the names of all the martyrs who were burnt at the stake only 200 yards from the cross. Robert Glover is named on that memorial, and in Mancetter Church there are two beautiful plaques – one to Robert Glover the Martyr and the other to Carol Lewis, a friend of the Glover family who also perished the same way as Robert two years later. That is some inheritance to be proud of, and although there were no martyrs in my family's background it gave both Ian and me a most interesting ancestry! I have since read Foxe's *Book of Martyrs* outlining the history of Robert Glover and, sadly, it was the older brother, John, the sheriff was after, not Robert.

So now, here I was on the threshold of perhaps finding

Mancetter Manor, Warwickshire home to the Glover family for over 100 years. Ian's Ancestor, Robert Glover, was taken from here in 1555, tried in Lichfield and burnt at the stake in Coventry for his beliefs. He was made a Martyr and is mentioned in Foxe's Book of Martyrs.

another lost sister if she, too, was still alive! From an only child I had discovered what had happened to four out of five of my half-siblings, which in itself was amazing and something I had never anticipated. Where was the road ahead going to take me now? Even if I found the sixth child of Vera's, there were still huge gaps in my birth mother's 'life plan' when nothing was known about where she went, what she did or whom she was with, apart from one spell around the early nineteen-seventies. There are great gaps in her timeline still unknown about her whereabouts or experiences.

In November 2017, I received the information that my adoption team believed they had found my missing sister! Again, it is quite unbelievable that this had worked. I had to travel to Birmingham for a face-to-face interview, as no information could be given by letter or telephone and personal interviews were the only permitted contact due to current data protection once more. And so it was with some butterflies in my stomach, that I once again ascended the stairs to After Adoptions to discover what they knew and could reveal about my missing sister.

I have to relate that my experiences with this team were absolutely wonderful and handled in such a humane and kind way. Even at that interview I was not given any personal information about my sister, even her new name or where she was. It was simply a precautionary interview to ensure that I wished to continue and give permission for them to pursue the matter on my behalf, which of course I gladly gave! They had their own way of contacting people, and now it was once again the waiting game. I left the office feeling very mixed emotions, looking at the sky and wondering where under that canopy my missing sister was, and realising what a shock she might be about to receive!

However, I did not have to wait very long. The team contacted my sister, who lived in Ireland and she reacted immediately, wishing to be put in touch with me. All the practicalities of the way to move forward were related to me and it was advised that first of all I should send a letter to 'Janet' – this being the name she was given upon adoption, which I did immediately. A letter from Janet came straight back to me! We felt we needed to speak to each other and this was sanctioned by the team in Birmingham and I have to say that since that day we have never stopped talking to each other! It is as if parallel lives have been lived by us in total ignorance of each other, and we have so many similar ideas, personality and outlook. Even our thought processes seem to work along the same lines many times when we are chatting or discussing what we wish to do regarding our lost family.

How strange coincidences (or fate, if people believe in it) can be. Janet lives in Ireland as, of course, does Carolyn. Two sisters, living only fifty-six miles apart, for thirty-two years and yet never knew each other existed in sixty-five years! If only for this in itself I am so thankful I pursued the matter of my long-lost family and have given two sisters each other to enjoy, hopefully, now for many years!

Janet has not had a particularly easy life, but she and I are so alike in some of our experiences and definitely in the way we think! We feel we have known each other all our lives, not just a few months! We can talk for ages on the phone about all sorts of things, and usually have a conversation every couple of days to 'catch up'. All sorts of questions arise of course, and we try to help by bouncing ideas and questions off each other.

As was the case with Hazel, myself and Bobby, Janet was taken from our birth mother shortly after her birth and fostered with lovely people, Mr and Mrs Brown, who then adopted the child when she was three years old. In the months following our connection, Janet managed to obtain her adoption file (after tremendous difficulties), which revealed much the same information about our birth mother as I had previously discovered from my care papers and which Kirstie had discovered from her mother, Hazel's, care papers. There are still many unanswered questions and we hope to discover more in due course, and are doing our best to follow up leads and get clarification of certain things.

Janet actually met our birth mother, Vera, in the early 1970s. In order to do so she had to be interviewed by social services three separate times. At one of those interviews she was told at least three pieces of information which she has wondered about ever since. Upon receiving her care file she thought she would receive clarification of those matters, but nothing revealing is contained in the file she actually received which had any connection with her queries whatsoever. It is made very difficult indeed for anyone to obtain their own care papers, which does seem ridiculous. Maybe the information she was told was from another file – perhaps our birth mother's, in which case the secrecy is understandable. She is therefore currently attempting to discover whether there is another 'pre-adoption' file (which is possible) or where those snippets of information came from. We are all keeping our fingers crossed that she will trace these and receive the clarification she is desperate for.

We all have experienced what Janet said when we were discussing her attempts to meet our birth mother. 'I wish I had listened more and taken in much more information about what I was told. But of course I was young and was more focused on actually meeting Vera than listening carefully or taking notes of what I was told.'

Janet met our birth mother in approximately 1975 or 1976 when she was in her twenties. At the time Vera was living in Crewe, Cheshire, with a man who made it quite clear that Janet was not wanted there. 'We don't need this,' he said, and told Janet that he was soon to marry Vera. Apparently, Vera did not speak at all, but gave Janet two small jigsaw puzzles for her children and Janet simply left after around ten minutes as the situation was so uncomfortable. She regrets this so much, as she would have loved to speak to Vera, but it was not meant to be. Thankfully I have managed to send Janet photographs and a bit of video footage of times my family and I met Vera, and we are sharing all sorts of information as we build our relationship as sisters.

Janet also had to run the gauntlet of meeting our grandparents as well as enduring these three interviews before she was allowed to go ahead and meet Vera. We do not know why this was the case, but she said that our grandparents, Martha and Thomas, were then living in Saighton Village. She met them two or three times and tells me they were such lovely people; particularly Grandad Ashton, and it is so nice to think that at least one of Vera's children met our grandparents.

Janet has told me that her parents, Mr and Mrs Brown, having firstly had children of their own, still fostered many other children despite them approaching their sixties and even seventies, and it is obvious from Janet's care papers how much they loved and wanted this little baby girl. It is really heart-warming to realise what wonderful people there are who take unwanted children into their homes and lives. My sister even remembers going to Kilrie Home with her foster mother in order to collect a child who needed fostering care – I wonder if I was one of those babies for a short time. Who knows?

And so the story goes on. In my seventieth year I can look back with wonderment at how my life has unfolded, the people I have known, what I have discovered and the apparently never-ending story of my birth family. The saddest thing is that it is extremely unlikely I will ever be able to discover anything about my birth father. It would have been wonderful to know something about him, what part of Italy he came from, etc. My Italian ancestry from him was confirmed with my DNA test. Several good friends have vague ideas of pathways I could try, so 'never say never' – that 'old wooden spoon' is still stirring up many things between my siblings and myself hitherto never even thought of before, and we keep storing information and ideas between us …

Unless further papers relating to myself, Janet or Bobby are discovered, it is unlikely much more will be uncovered about our pasts, but when papers are received they inevitably open up another Pandora's Box. Also, of course, Bobby's carers are desperate to acquire his lifelong care papers which could help them understand things he tries to tell them and could possibly reveal more about our birth mother (or even ourselves) to us.

We are not one hundred percent certain whether there could be another sibling (or siblings) somewhere in the world. The first time we spoke to one another by telephone Janet asked me how many of us there were. Upon telling her I knew there were six she told me she seemed to remember that the social worker back in the 1970s told her there were seven – five girls and two boys! We don't know whether this is true, or whether Janet misheard the information, and it is one of the queries we all have.

What an incredible year my seventieth has proved to be, so hopefully there will be one more chapter to be entered in this bizarre and (seemingly) never-ending story when the sister I have never known in my seventy years even existed and, at long last, meet for the very first time.

Whether there be a 'definite' conclusion to this adventure in the next chapter is debatable, and I may have to leave it open 'just in case'.

Never say never, for I do believe if things are meant to be – they will be.

CHAPTER 20

A Dream Come True ...

———

The year 2018 was indeed an exceptional and very special one. It felt quite an achievement to reach the 'seventy' milestone, and special birthday celebrations in February were the kickstart to begin this outstanding year when so many people from all parts of my life gathered with me to enjoy two wonderful buffet parties. There was a mixture of dear friends made over the past few years, going back to one very special lady, Brenda, who at ten years older than myself remembered and played with me when I was a baby. Living in Lincolnshire she could not make the journey to either of my actual celebrations, so instead I went to visit her for a few days instead.

It was necessary to have two events – one in the Manchester area and the other in Wolverhampton, as distance prevented the whole group meeting up in one place. Catching up with so many amazing people was something completely out of this world and amongst the guests in Wolverhampton was an aunt, uncle and two cousins from my birth family. Who could have imagined such a thing could ever have happened?

I had only recently met my first-cousin, Joseph, who is one of my Aunt Joan's sons – the aunt being Vera's older sister who sadly died at the age of forty-seven.

How wonderful it was to see all these friends again, but even so I realised just how many were no longer with us. That is a true sign of the times, but I was so fortunate so many were still able to attend. My daughters attended both celebrations and so did the majority of my grandchildren, which was lovely.

In Wolverhampton my celebrations were held at the golf club where Gerald had been treasurer for some years, and quite a few people went outside to look at his memorial cherry tree and plaque, which was nice. Auntie Betty and Uncle Eric, being the two surviving siblings of my birth mother, were also there but sadly we lost Auntie Betty a few months later. I miss her a lot. Uncle Eric lives in Chester not too far from my youngest daughter, and I try to visit him whenever I go to see Helen.

What wonderful memories I have of those two occasions, with a lot of memorabilia to keep, photographs and videos. It is sad that my two sisters in Ireland were not able to come to these celebrations, but even so we were already looking forward to our arranged meeting later in the year.

In July these festivities were followed by a fascinating Baltic cruise including a day in St Petersburg, which is a place never in my wildest dreams I could have imagined visiting at all!

Throughout every single month there were visits, trips and interesting people 'catching up', and then in September Janet and I decided it was high time to actually meet. Time was not particularly on our side (especially mine), and it would be a full year soon before we had shared our first telephone conversation in November 2017. It was therefore decided that I would take my car over to Ireland in October 2018 for a few days so that Carolyn, Janet and I could meet and be together for the very first time.

What excitement this caused and, as neither of my daughters were able to accompany me, my friend Maureen was so happy to keep me company on the journeys, so on the 2nd of October Maureen and I sailed over to Ireland from Birkenhead to Belfast. I had a little bit of trepidation about the ferry (an eight-hour sail), but although I had to put my car right on the top deck of the ship it was fine and thankfully went without any problems. With only a short journey from the docks in Belfast to our bed and breakfast venue in Bangor, we arrived safely.

Waking up on the 3rd of October, this was going to be the day of days: I was about to meet – for the very first time in my life – my long-lost younger sister Janet.

Of course I had met our other sister, Carolyn, back in 1995 after extensive research, but at that time we had no idea there were three siblings we knew nothing whatsoever about! This meeting was to be the culmination of months of telephone conversations, research, feeling impatient and never imagining that life would throw up even more revealing situations so far along in our lives.

Maureen and I were staying at a lovely bed and breakfast in Bangor, Northern Ireland called the Shellevan Guest House, which was absolutely beautiful and so comfortable. After a delicious breakfast, Maureen and I drove over to Cookstown to collect Carolyn, and together we attended the Strangford Arms Hotel in Carrowdore, Newtownard's, where Janet had booked a room for two hours to enable us to meet privately for the very first time.

I took my camcorder with me to record these very special, emotional and never-to-be repeated happenings, but for the actual time when Janet would enter the room one of her friends called Noel kindly said he would borrow my video camera to record the very first meeting for us, and he did a grand job!

We were due to meet Janet at the Strangford Arms (quite nervously) at 2 p.m. that special day so we had to ensure we arrived an hour or so early. When Maureen, Carolyn and I were shown into the room at the hotel, we discovered a little fairy called Janet had been in earlier and the room was beautifully decorated and prepared for this very special occasion with balloons, photographs, a fabulous cake, banners and lovely words on posters around the room.. There were two

3rd October 2018. Three long-lost sisters met for the very first time.
Left to right: Carolyn, Judith and Janet.

enormous bouquets of beautiful flowers for both Carolyn and myself, and two smaller bouquets for my friend Maureen and Janet's friend Claire, who was to accompany Janet to the meeting for support! Janet had obviously been preparing for weeks beforehand and royalty could not have been treated any better – she really went the extra mile.

Janet's husband, Tom, was the first to come into the room, followed by Janet, whose arms were full of the flowers. It was simply amazing when we saw each other for the first time, but Carolyn completely lost it and sobbed her heart out whilst embracing Janet. She went to Janet like a magnet! It was so lovely to witness, and we spent quite a while all trying to talk at the same time. Around ten minutes later my friend Maureen, Janet's friend Claire and one or two other people came in to join us and it was such a wonderful time – so happy, and completely unbelievable. No directions as to where to sit or feeling uncomfortable pressured by television cameras. Carolyn would not have wanted to be on television anyway, as she became really overwhelmed at the occasion and was later seen eating lots of cake (at a point she didn't realise she was being filmed!). We were all relaxed and so it was a moment in history genuinely recorded.

It was one of those times when the hours seemed to fly by and quite a surreal feeling to see three sisters – one of them a complete stranger to the other two, meet up for the very first time ever. And yet there was no stumbling, strangeness or shyness. It was just as if we had all known each other for years.

It wasn't too long before the local newspaper reporter and photographer from the Newtownard's Chronicle turned up at three o'clock. They had run a piece on our special occasion a couple of weeks before by interviewing Janet on her own, and now wanted Part Two. Obviously they wished to interview Carolyn and myself, so we did a short interview and I provided a written account in an attempt to help them understand the very intricate and bizarre story of our reunion. It was difficult to explain forty years of searching in an hour. The photographer from the newspaper took a lot of photographs as well as myself and other people. He took a short video which was placed on the newspaper's website, and I believe we had around 2,000 'hits' on it. Fame at last!

Needless to say we never stopped talking and at 4 p.m. we all trooped down to the restaurant where Janet had booked a beautiful meal for us. The waiter became very interested and started taking photographs of us on his mobile phone, and then after the meal the manager of the Strangford Arms came with a lovely complimentary bottle of champagne to round the afternoon off.

We spent the remainder of the evening and the following day at Janet's home, sharing our personal memories and trying to make sense of the different bits of information we all had regarding our different upbringings and what we each knew about ourselves and our birth mother. Obviously, there are still many questions we would love answers to, but for now we have more than enough to satisfy us in the fact that three sisters were together for the very first time in their lives at the ages of seventy, sixty-six and fifty-nine.

Carolyn stayed overnight with Janet for two nights which meant they had plenty of time to discuss things and get to know each other, which was lovely. Hopefully they will be able to visit and spend time together in the future. Janet actually invited Carolyn to spend Christmas 2018 with Tom and herself, which she did, and I believe they had a marvellous time together.

Maureen and I returned to England on the 5th of October and, like my two sisters, I am still trying hard to come back down to earth and sort out the emotions, bonds and elation at what we have all found so late in life. It still seems so surreal at times! We intend to still try researching things we believe to be true but have no evidence of, and are really looking forward, hopefully, to having many years yet together as sisters.

And so I have reached my seventies. This is a time of my life which is so wonderful, with lovely, thoughtful and caring daughters, grandchildren, great-grandchildren and wonderful friends. Of course families all experience difficulties sometimes, and no one's life can be one hundred percent perfect all the time as sad and upsetting events also happen alongside the good. Not all members of families remain in touch all their lives, but I have no complaints or regrets whatsoever, and that is something many people cannot say so I have been extremely lucky and blessed. It seems I am related to half of England when I look at my newly-found family, and if I knew about my Italian father I would probably discover I was related to half of Italy as well! Perhaps I will try to discover the region of my paternal birth family at some time through ancestry, as that in itself would be fascinating to know.

I could never complain about missing out regarding travel, as just so many of those places in my childhood 'Encyclopaedia' have now been visited in person, including a visit to India at the end of 2018 and actually experiencing the wonderful Taj Mahal! My travelling companion, John, is hoping to make further travel arrangements whilst we still have the health and ability to do so.

Since meeting in 2018, Janet, Carolyn and I have been in constant communication, and I have been over to Ireland again, and long may this continue. We get on so well, and it is still unbelievable that we had to wait for so long to discover each other. Still, better late than never!

I wonder what the future may still hold – more discoveries?

CHAPTER 21

Where Do We Go From Here?

———

I must be one of the luckiest people in the world to have seen so much, discovered so much in my own life and to have such a lovely family. At home my life is completely filled with memories of the two wonderful men I have shared my life with, busy with writing, groups, interests and many friends who virtually all came to the two celebration buffets for my seventieth birthday.

There is still an outside possibility of us having a seventh sibling, but despite extensive research, visits to archives, trawling ancestry sites and hoping perhaps something may be revealed in other files, if they can ever be traced, we have no notion of whether she (or, indeed, possibly others) exist. Without names, positive dates or information revealed in files we are not currently being allowed to read, this research is impossible. Still, I shall never give up, and as I have discovered in the past it is amazing how something can suddenly appear! Certainly that old wooden spoon may currently lie dormant in a drawer, but it can still stir – so who knows?

Now and then people ask me how it feels to have unexpectedly discovered all these unusual and unexpected family members and the only way I can describe it is to say that it is almost like looking on at someone else's life – as if it is all happening to someone else.

I hope I have not bored the reader with this book, and trust they find it interesting and unusual. It would seem now that the conclusion has been reached, but thinking about how things can suddenly occur and appear out of nowhere I am not one hundred percent certain, and of course Janet, myself and other 'new' family members are still awaiting (hopefully) more papers. Also, Bobby's carers hope for his history so goodness knows what might be revealed if we can fulfil these wishes, although because of time lapse and attempting to discover what has been retained, archived or remembered there may be nothing more to find. The present day situations of data protection and freedom of information seem to cancel each other out and make searching far more difficult, but persistence can sometimes help. People even find it difficult now to discover information about themselves, which seems ridiculous, and is something I have been up against quite a few times during my searches.

Of course, Frank Sinatra sang about doing it all 'his way', and really most of us have done just that, with a few blips along the road. We can forgive those who have treated us with cruelty or injustice, but it is much harder to forget than forgive. However revisiting hurtful times in the past does not achieve anything except continued heartache, and all that can be hoped for is that anyone who has instigated such unfairness will come to their senses and attempt to retrieve some semblance of communication before it is too late. Looking backwards only ensures we will crash into something and carry regrets in our backpacks. Life is far too short for such burdens, so looking to the present and the future is always best. It seems that as people age they become quite philosophical, having been through tough times, experienced life and generally (hopefully) learnt from the past.

I cannot equate that timid, shy, awkward little girl who was an only child with the person I have become, or indeed believe the life which has unfolded with all its twists, turns and discoveries. Definitely the unexpected outcome of finding my birth family and most, if not all, the truth about what happened. In some ways I was lucky to be given the childhood home I remember so well, despite not realising the negativity and – sometimes – negligence which accompanied it. It was a happy but lonely childhood in many ways, and certainly I was never given the opportunity to think for myself in any way shape or form, which made adult life very hard for many years. But those formative years taught me so much about how 'not' to bring my own family up, and to this day my one regret is that not once in my lifetime, whilst my mother was still alive, did I ever have an 'adult' conversation with her. I see friends who have always been 'pals' with their mums, shared things and been so close. That would have been so lovely – for mothers and daughters to be 'friends' in adulthood. How different it *could* have been, for I am certain she had the love inside her but sadly was far too dominated and insecure herself to realise how things were.

I still feel sadness for my dad, who would have done so much if allowed, made Mum a different person and lived a much happier life for himself if she had only given him the chance, instead of tying herself to Gran, who was a dominating person quite capable of being independent as she was talented, clever and very overbearing. The Victorian era shaped her and obviously she had a hard upbringing, which made her the person she was – we cannot judge as there is no knowledge of the privations and difficulties she herself experienced.

And so life moves (or grinds) on and we never know what is around the corner, which of course the dreadful Coronavirus in this year of 2020 has proved. I was actually on the cruise ships *Vaandam* and *Rotterdam* during this period on a South American holiday, which was a heart-breaking experience, but proved that every day is a journey to be highly valued and every moment to be treasured. If humanity learns anything from this tragedy, hopefully it is to respect and care for each other. The past cannot be changed, but the present and the future can. Life is far too delicate to harbour grudges, and sadly thousands of people have now learnt it is too late to say 'sorry'. Certainly the 'present' is a gift.

Reaching the age of seventy and beyond (if one is lucky enough) makes a person very philosophical, but it is a matter of using that old 'brain computer' to find ways around problems to keep active mentally and physically and as in tune with the current years as possible. Accept change, for if my life has taught me one thing it is that problems, and being treated unjustly or cruelly, cannot be avoided. However, the unexpected can happen at any time, be it good or bad, and life holds many amazing and incredible wonders – from the birth of our children, the love of relatives and friends, and nature's unfolding magic.

The universe is still turning, secrets can still unfold, and it may be a matter of 'watch this space' even now. Who knows?

Thank you for reading my book.
J. Glover 2020

Me and my girls. Left to right: Margaret, myself and Helen.